I BELIEVE IN ZERO

ALSO BY CARYL M. STERN
(and Ellen Hofheimer Bettmann)

*Hate Hurts: How Children Learn
and Unlearn Prejudice*

I BELIEVE IN ZERO
Learning from the World's Children

Caryl M. Stern
President and CEO of the U.S. Fund for UNICEF

Foreword by Téa Leoni

ST. MARTIN'S PRESS
NEW YORK

www.stmartins.com

"I Believe in ZERO" is a registered trademark owned by, and is used here by permission of, the U.S. Fund for UNICEF.

Library of Congress Cataloging-in-Publication Data

Stern, Caryl M.
  I believe in ZERO : learning from the world's children / by Caryl M. Stern, President & CEO of the U.S. Fund for UNICEF.
        pages cm
    ISBN 978-1-250-02624-8 (hardcover)
    ISBN 978-1-250-02625-5 (e-book)
  1. Children's rights.   2. Children—Social conditions.   I. Title.
    HQ789.S757 2013
    305.23—dc23

                                                                            2013013661

St. Martin's Press books may be purchased for educational, business, or promotional use. For information on bulk purchases, please contact Macmillan Corporate and Premium Sales Department at 1-800-221-7945, extension 5442, or write specialmarkets@macmillan.com.

First Edition: October 2013

10 9 8 7 6 5 4 3 2 1

This book is dedicated to my UNICEF colleagues on the ground and around the globe, who put their lives at risk on behalf of children, every day.

AUTHOR'S NOTE

This book was written as a personal story. It is based upon my own experiences, my memory of those experiences, and the perceptions I have formed as a result. It is not to be construed as a UNICEF publication or a U.S. Fund for UNICEF publication. I have chosen to direct 100 percent of royalties I would otherwise receive to the U.S. Fund for UNICEF to benefit vulnerable children around the world. For more information, please visit unicefusa.org/bookroyalties.

CONTENTS

ACKNOWLEDGMENTS

If it takes a village to raise a child, it takes a universe to write about it. Thank you to Seth Schulman, who helped me to find the right words to tell my stories and whose editing of my writing helped them to come alive. Thank you to my agent, Lorin Rees, for believing in the project, and to George Witte and all the folks at St. Martin's Press for sharing that belief. I am forever indebted to my dear friends and colleagues Brian Meyers, Emily Distel, Lisa Szarkowski, and Harry Wall. Their research, their additions, their willingness to read every word again and again (as well as the fact that they kept me laughing throughout the year of writing) were invaluable. Finally, thank you to the people who make me who I am: to my mom and dad, Manny and Edwin Stern, as well as to my brother, Mitchell Stern, who made our home a place where we learned to care about the world around us. To my husband, Donald, who not only kept the light on at home as I ran around the world, but whose arms welcomed me back each time. To my sons, Brian, Lee, and James, who accepted that work often kept me from being home at the end of the day, and to my friend Naomi, who listens to it all and helps me balance it. All of you have made possible the journey that has now become this book. I love you all.

FOREWORD

by Téa Leoni

ACTRESS TÉA LEONI is a third-generation member of the UNICEF family. Her grandmother Helenka Pantaleoni cofounded the U.S. Fund for UNICEF in 1947 and served as its president for twenty-five years. Anthony Pantaleoni, Téa's father, is an active member of the U.S. Fund for UNICEF's board of directors, serving as board chair from 2008 to 2012.

Though Téa has been a UNICEF volunteer since childhood, her formal service began in 2001, when she was named UNICEF ambassador. In 2006 she was elected to the U.S. Fund for UNICEF national board. She continues in both roles and has been a tireless fund-raiser and advocate for the world's children in support of UNICEF's mission.

Heroes wear capes.

Capes are for those who dare to leap from tall buildings or pull stranded cats out of towering trees. The ones who always land on their never-tired feet, and whose story always ends with white teeth gleaming in a glory shot.

But there is no cape here, not for this author.

Because Caryl Stern didn't write this book as a hero, she

wrote it as a mother. And like every mother in the world, she loves her children above all else. She would carry them down a mountain for air, she would find them in the middle of the farthest desert, and she would make the first flight back from anywhere to be with them when they needed her. You'll read more about that later. . . .

Caryl came to the U.S. Fund for UNICEF for another job and became the president of the organization six months later. She came as an accomplished defender of human rights and quickly proved to be an outspoken and outstanding advocate for children. She also came without any field experience and a very pronounced, irrational fear of bugs (the latter of which has entertained every one of us who has ever had the chance to travel with her).

But it is Caryl's strength as a mother that guides her eyes and ears and heart in these pages.

She writes about what it is to face another mother's loss or a child's pain when there is no chance to turn away or turn it off, and of the awesome and constant strength of the human spirit that she has witnessed in conditions most of us could never even imagine. She writes about the day she saw a mother in the middle of the desert and they shared an apple from New York, and the day she stood by and held the hand of a new mother as her baby took its last breath.

She doesn't write as some kind of fearless hero with all the answers, leaving pages full of solutions and cures in her wake. She tells these stories with a kind of honest humility that is rare.

She admits to missing the hot showers of home, to feeling ashamed of not doing enough, to being afraid—whether for her own life amid the aftershocks in Haiti, or just of something crawling into her tent. And she writes of wanting to get home to her children, like every mother in the world.

There isn't a need to exaggerate the plight of millions of women and children around the world, but there is always the need for an honest and powerful witness.

Caryl is that witness, because she isn't just reporting what she sees, she is telling us what is there.

On one of her earliest trips, to Sudan, Caryl made a promise to those she met in one of the camps, that she would use her voice "to tell their stories and to get others to listen." These are their stories.

After reading this book, I realized that perhaps more than anything else, Caryl has written about why we must believe in zero.

Because these are not *their* children, they are all *our* children, each and every one. As for the cape? I may know better, but I bet there are children out there in the world that would love to peek into Caryl's duffel bag to see where she keeps hers.

I BELIEVE IN ZERO

1. ROSA'S WALK

Mozambique, January 2007

REGARDLESS OF WHERE I HAVE TRAVELED, to a major city in an industrialized country or a small remote village in a developing nation, I have found three things to be true.

First, where I see children, there will be some sort of ball. Sometimes the ball is made of rubber or plastic, often just rags held together by twine, but always I see a child tossing it or kicking it and at least one other child returning it in much the same fashion.

Second, my lap is not my personal property. If I plop down on the ground and sit patiently, a child will eventually find his or her way onto my lap.

Third, and most important, parents everywhere want the same things for their children. We want them to be healthy. To be safe. To feel loved. To have an education. To dream big dreams and have a fighting chance to realize those dreams. This is the same everywhere in the world, no matter how much people have to eat, how accessible education may be, or whether the community has running water, electricity, or basic health care. We each define success differently, but as parents, we all want the best for our children.

It was in Mozambique, at a birthing clinic, that I first met Rosa. The site was accessible only by a rutted dirt road, so far from stoplights or street signs or any other markers that I marveled the driver of our jeep had even found it. The clinic was a primitive structure composed of two rooms, a birthing room and a maternity ward. It did have walls, windows, electricity, and running water—four things I had rarely seen as we had driven through the countryside. Still, no air-conditioning or ceiling fan, only the relief that comes from being inside and thus shaded from direct sunlight. It was hot, stifling, hard to breathe.

Entering the birthing room, I found little more than a table with stirrups and another, smaller table holding a few basic medical instruments. In the ward, ten narrow metal beds were arranged side by side, covered with billowy mosquito nets hanging from the ceiling. I found no place to sit, save a lone metal chair stowed in a corner—an indication that visitors were not expected.

There were no doctors. No registered nurses. No professionally trained and educated midwives. In this corner of the world, babies were delivered and mothers attended to either at home surrounded by family members or by health-care workers with the equivalent of a sixth-grade education.

Rosa lay resting on her bed, draped with a colorful sheet. She had given birth an hour earlier; her beautiful baby girl lay beside her. Observing them, I remembered the summer heat I had felt years earlier when pregnant with my youngest son, James. The humid New York City air had seemed to envelop me as I tried to get through my day, step by difficult step. And yet, here was Rosa with eight other women, none of whom seemed bothered by the heat at all.

On Rosa's face I detected the combination of exhaustion

and exhilaration that those of us who have delivered children know so well. A large-boned woman, very dark-skinned, short hair in braids, she had delivered her daughter naturally, lacking access to pain medications or any type of anesthesia.

I wanted so badly to hear what the women in this ward were thinking and feeling, and since Rosa's was the only bed without its bed net tightly drawn, I came close to her and nodded hello. I wasn't sure how to begin a conversation. What do you say to a woman unknown to you who has just gone through the intensely personal, not to mention emotional and physical, ordeal of giving birth?

I came up with something innocuous yet friendly. Smiling down at her, I asked, "Is this your first child?"

She answered so matter-of-factly—in such a neutral tone— that at first I was not sure I had fully understood or that the interpreter had gotten it right. "The first one that lived."

And so my education began.

I had never experienced a place like Mozambique before, nor had the realities of developing countries ever really entered my awareness. Raised during the 1960s in the northern part of Westchester County, New York, I enjoyed a typical middle-class, suburban upbringing. My dad was a podiatrist, my mom a homemaker and real estate broker. We lived in a relatively large home on a beautiful block, attended local schools, and worried about very little.

The closest I got to "roughing it" was spending part of each summer at a Jewish sleepaway camp in the Pocono Mountains. During my twenties, I dated a boy who was an avid camper and whose ideal weekend included spur-of-the-moment treks in the woods. He would cheerily put up the tent and then grab a bath in a cold lake; I indulged my anxieties by spraying bug repellent everywhere (I have long had an extreme fear of mosquitoes and spiders). His only concession to me: campsites with latrines. Much to the amusement of his friends and their girlfriends, I was more of a princess than I had ever realized. Not exactly a desirable character trait for someone who would end up working in remote areas of developing nations.

A year before meeting Rosa, I doubt I would have even been able to find Mozambique on a map. I had just turned fifty and spent the better part of eighteen years working for the Anti-Defamation League. Wanting more opportunity, I applied for a position as chief operating officer that had opened up at the U.S. Fund for UNICEF (United Nations Children's Fund). The U.S. Fund's president and CEO, Chip Lyons, was looking for someone who could run the organization's day-to-day operations while he focused on global issues. As I listened to him expand upon his vision and recount his vast overseas experience, I began to picture myself working there. My mind was filled with images of myself in remote locations, experiencing the things Chip was describing—opportunities I had only dreamed of. I had a minimal understanding of what poverty really was or what it meant to live in a developing nation, but the pictures were enticing enough, and I was honored to accept Chip's offer to join his team.

Three weeks into my new job, just as I was getting my bearings at the U.S. Fund, Chip called me into his office, shut the door, and told me we needed to talk. Wondering what I had done wrong, I almost missed what he was saying. He had been offered and had accepted a phenomenal opportunity with the Bill & Melinda Gates Foundation—a dream come true for someone trying to improve the world for children. He would be leaving the U.S. Fund in a few short months. I was stunned, unsure what this meant for my own future. As I caught my breath, I realized he was encouraging me to apply for the top job that he occupied.

I looked at him like he was crazy. "I don't know. I have never even visited the countries UNICEF serves. I have no firsthand knowledge of the work on the ground. I am not sure I understand the issues, much less the solutions. How could the board even consider me?" What I didn't say was that I also wondered if I had the temperament for Chip's job. Chip excelled at diplomacy, adopting a subtle, almost European style in his handling of people. I was more typically American—direct, loud, and proud. At the very least, I would need some coaching.

Chip insisted I could learn what I needed to take on his role, and he offered to mentor me. In the weeks before his departure, we met daily. He gave me stacks of files, books, reports, and other documents to read. And videos—hours and hours of tapes. I'd read and watch, and then we'd talk. The plan was to top off all this work with a trip to the field to see firsthand all I had been learning about. Chip and I and two USF board members would go to Mozambique—a large East African country where Chip had previously lived. He would arrange an itinerary that would expose me directly to the effects of severe poverty on mothers and children, as well as to the role UNICEF plays in meeting those challenges.

I surprised myself by feeling nervous. I had traveled for work in my previous jobs, yet I had never visited Africa or experienced the conditions of a developing country. What shots would I need? What would I eat in Mozambique? Would the travel vaccinations sicken me? What about the bugs? Mostly, though, I worried about how I would do professionally. Would I be emotionally strong enough to maintain my professionalism in the face of all that I would see and experience? How would I react to the sights, the smells, the diseases? Would I be able to witness human suffering with my own eyes, process it, and find the words to talk about it afterward?

We had landed in Maputo, Mozambique's capital, a few days before I met Rosa. In a briefing at UNICEF's offices, I learned some basic facts about the country. Like other developing countries, Mozambique's population is young, with children under the age of eighteen accounting for half of the country's 20 million people. Mozambique ranks among the world's twenty poorest countries, near the bottom in development. The country relies on international aid for half its national budget, making it Africa's single biggest recipient of international aid. Almost half the country's children live in extreme poverty, lacking access to adequate sanitation, clean water, schooling, and other basics of life.

I heard these facts but was not sure I fully grasped their meaning. Leila Pakkala, the UNICEF country representative in Mozambique, summarized them in a way that made a strong impression: "Mozambique's children are like any other group of young people. They have hopes and aspirations. But it is like their whole childhood is being robbed because of poverty." Leila also gave us a bit of history. As poor as Mozambique currently is, things had been improving. Sixteen years of devastating civil war had ended in 1992, and despite the horrific effects of periodic droughts and extreme floods, Mozambique's economy had grown at a strong 9 percent annual pace, pulling almost 20 percent of the population up from poverty.[1]

As Leila's colleague, the chief of education for our Mozambique team, pointed out, important improvements in the country's education system had led to significant increases in enrollment and attendance rates, with 81 percent of children ages six to twelve years now going to school. I was especially happy to hear this. The power of education is a basic tenet of my professional life, best summarized in a quote that goes roughly like this: "If we solve all the problems of the world but fail to solve the problems of education, our children will destroy what we bequeath them. But, if we solve only the problems of education, our children will solve the problems of the world." I think it was Thomas Jefferson who first uttered this idea, but I'm not sure. Whatever the case, I believe in that statement. Education is the only tool in our arsenal that can truly interrupt the cycle of poverty.

As positive as some of these developments had been, a terrible new challenge had emerged: HIV/AIDS. As the health officers on our Mozambique team told me, almost 2 million people—10 percent of Mozambique's population—had AIDS or were HIV-positive as of 2007, the majority of them women. I was saddened to hear that a quarter of the country's orphans had lost their parents to AIDS. How would Mozambique ever be able to emerge out of poverty if it couldn't overcome the human toll and economic burden that HIV/AIDS was exacting? I had lost friends to AIDS, watching once-vibrant lives dwindle.

As the briefing concluded, I tried to imagine being a young child watching my parents succumb to HIV/AIDS—even worse, having them experience it without common pain medications, antibiotics, or government social services. I also tried to picture what life in New York City would be like if one in every ten people contracted the disease. That was almost unfathomable.

The Plight of Mozambique's Children, 2007

Over half of Mozambique's population lived in poverty.

Over 10 percent of children died in infancy.

Fully 41 percent of children were stunted by poor nutrition.

380,000 children had both parents die from AIDS.

Almost 40 percent of women ages fifteen to nineteen were married.

Only 28 percent of women could read, as opposed to 67 percent of men.

Almost half of all children had no access to a toilet near their home.

Almost a quarter of children ages seven to eighteen had never been to school.

Source: UNICEF, Mozambique country office; press release, Rachel Bonham Carter, "Report Finds Nearly Half of All Children in Mozambique Living in Extreme Poverty," December 14, 2006.

We flew to Beira, Mozambique's second largest city and the epicenter of its HIV/AIDS epidemic, to visit several UNICEF projects on the ground. At the Manga-Mascarenhas Health Center, we saw one of the few permanent medical facilities in the country dedicated to meeting the needs of malnourished children. Children brought to the center were screened, and severely malnourished children were able to take home with them a supply of Plumpy'Nut, a peanut butter–like food packed with calories and essential nutrients. Meanwhile, counselors helped mothers understand how to make a nutrient-filled porridge for their children to eat. The Manga-Mascarenhas facility had just opened, and more were in the works for other cities in Mozambique. UNICEF hoped that the center would cut down the number of children who were dying of malnutrition and also provide a place for children to be tested for HIV.[2] I found it really encouraging to see such a concrete example of progress on the ground, even if it was disconcerting to see firsthand evidence of human suffering and poverty.

Next I got a chance to witness what UNICEF and other NGOs were doing to fight cholera and diarrhea, water-borne diseases that hit young children. UNICEF had been helping the government of Mozambique build essential water and sanitation infrastructures—the kind of thing that we take for granted in places like the United States because in our lifetimes we've always had it. We saw workers clearing out drainage canals so that floods that hit the area would recede more quickly, thereby posing less of a health threat. Other workers were building waterworks to bring clean water to schools. Our colleagues told us about still other efforts to build more sanitary latrines in household areas, as well as projects aimed at teaching the population about hand washing and other hygienic practices.[3]

All of this came as a real revelation to me. I had never considered that the water pouring forth from my sink tap was a luxury beyond the grasp of millions of people. Nor had I ever stopped to think what a difference something as simple as hand washing can make in lowering the number of children who take ill, or for that matter, who die. When I was a child, my mother constantly told me, "Wash your hands before you eat anything," so I had assumed this to be common practice everywhere. How incredible to think that for vast stretches of humanity, it wasn't.

We spent the next few days observing mobile health units, maternity clinics, and medical facilities serving rural areas. Leaving Beira, we drove north on EN 1, the main road—paved but heavily riddled with potholes—that hugs Mozambique's coast and runs through its middle. It was a rough ride, bouncing us up and down, leaving our backs aching and rear ends sore. Gazing out the window, I marveled at the massive, ancient baobab trees, whose thick trunks are hollow inside. The terrain was flat and seemed to stretch forever. Periodically, we passed people working in rice paddies and villages consisting of a few mud huts with thatched bamboo roofs. It was approaching 100 degrees Fahrenheit and extremely humid. I was grateful for the air-conditioning of the jeeps, even though you could feel the heat of the sun through the windows. I was also grateful to Dr. Roberto de Bernardi, a pediatrician on our Mozambique team, who as we drove told me stories about his life and conditions in Mozambique, including how few doctors the country had.

We entered isolated villages, and I saw with my own eyes just how meager the country's medical resources were. The first health clinic we visited was a one-room building with electricity but little else. Staff wrote out medical records by hand on pieces of paper. Many of the most basic medications, things like Tylenol or antibiotics, weren't available. Sometimes a doctor saw patients here, but usually health-care workers with limited education did that work, with patients waiting in very long lines for the privilege. The place stank of dirty diapers, vomit, and body odor, and we could hear children crying all around us.

Even a clinic like this was a luxury here; a great deal of medical care in Mozambique takes place in the absence of a fixed medical facility. At several points during our trip, we pulled up to a clearing in the bush to find a hundred or more people sitting on the ground or strolling around, quietly waiting for the health-care worker—in this case Roberto, in other cases a trained nurse—to arrive to see their children. These children and their families could receive only the basics, such as vitamin supplements, vaccinations, or deworming. For anything more serious, they would need to travel some distance to a clinic. Often the children were malnourished as a result of severe diarrhea, malaria, or respiratory infections.

Roberto showed me how the children were checked for malnutrition. First, they were weighed on a scale he had hung from a tree. The scale looked somewhat like the scales used to weigh fruit in a grocery store, except instead of a pan on which you'd place whatever it was you sought to weigh, there was a small pair of shorts. One by one, babies were placed in the shorts, dangling (often giggling, occasionally crying) as Roberto noted their weight. Next, the circumference of their arms was measured using a disposable, paper measuring tape. As I stood watching, Roberto did his best to charm the children and make them laugh, while someone took Polaroid pictures of the kids and gave them to their grateful mothers. A single, cherished Polaroid, the first and only picture of their child, compared to the brag book of photos I carried in my purse everywhere I went.

I found myself feeling a mix of emotions. I marveled at the sheer simplicity of what I was watching as well as at the deep respect shown to Roberto by the local residents. Still, I found it disturbing to compare health care here to what I enjoyed at home. I became frustrated when one of my kids fell ill and our family pediatrician couldn't see us immediately, yet these women would have to wait another month until Roberto or another health-care worker came to their corner of Mozambique. I went through bottles of baby Tylenol when my kids got a fever, gave them special ice pops to restore their electrolytes after a bout of diarrhea, and kept the kitchen drawer full of multicolored bandages, ready for placement on even the tiniest of boo-boos. What would these women think if

they could see all of that? And how would I react if I didn't
have these items available to me?

If life in Mozambique threw me off-balance, it also energized
me. I can't convey the sheer joy that washed over me as we
were welcomed into local villages. Each time we pulled up
in our jeeps, residents of all ages poured out of their huts and
surrounded us, singing and dancing, the women wearing
long, colorful dresses, the men and children often wearing
T-shirts printed with American slogans. I was particularly
amused at how many children wore the names of U.S. professional sports heroes emblazoned on their chests, with no
idea who these athletes were. The singing was warm and
sincere, and although I couldn't understand the words, the
melodious voices and wide smiles will stay with me always.

The first time I was welcomed into a village, I was so taken
with the beauty of the voices and the generosity of spirit our
hosts displayed that tears ran down my face. These celebra-
tions were truly an amazing gift being given to us. The
villagers might not have had anything to offer us in material terms, but in another, even more important sense they
had everything to give, and I felt blessed to receive it. I
laughed out loud—right through the tears—when Roberto
asked me if I could ever imagine the residents of my neigh-
borhood in suburban Bayside, Queens, offering such a welcome to a group of different-looking people, unexpectedly
pulling into town and taking pictures of all they were seeing. Unthinkable!

The great appreciation local residents had for UNICEF
also affected me. One night, our group was invited to experience an HIV/AIDS outreach program funded by UNICEF.

After bouncing around in our jeeps off-road in the pitch-black dark, we arrived at a large clearing in the bush. Once our eyes adjusted, we discovered hundreds of happy teenagers and young children spread out in front of us. Many had walked miles to sit on the ground here to watch a movie; few, if any, were wearing shoes of any kind. Between the heat and the darkness, I felt disoriented and nervous. All these people nearby—you could hear them moving and whispering, but you could barely see them through the darkness.

Without warning, a projector hooked up to a generator was turned on and a movie was projected onto a white bed-sheet hung between two poles. I had to squint, so bright was the light of the projector. A few minutes later, I glanced around and noticed a tent standing off to the side of the crowd, the opening not visible from where we were sitting. As the crowd was watching the movie, laughing and enjoying themselves, teens were quietly slipping off on their own to visit the tent. Curiosity got the best of me, and I walked over to see what was inside.

I found three adults, trained counselors, providing information about HIV/AIDS: where to get tested, the symptoms, how people could protect themselves. The counselors spoke freely with the young people, seeking them out, answering questions, and providing advice. I learned from my UNICEF colleagues that many of the kids in this area were living with the disease or assisting a loved one suffering from AIDS. The darkness of the night, the anonymity of the site, and the lack of required registration enabled these teens to get information they vitally needed without fear of social stigma.

In Mozambique, people with HIV/AIDS were considered outcasts. Many men refused to get tested or allow their wives to be tested, fearing what might happen if their wives were found to have the virus. As a few of the teens told me through an interpreter, many of their friends deemed testing unnecessary. Since there were scant treatment options available to them, why bother risking the stigma or living with the shame if you were found to be positive? Yet, inside the tent, I was pleased to see that some teens were being tested. Unfortunately, as my colleague later pointed out, some would never return to get the results.

I went back to watch the movie, noting how orderly the crowd was. Would hundreds of American kids gathered in any field or park at night sit so quietly? My colleagues and I sat in special lawn chairs set up for us as guests of honor, and the kids came over to say hello. Their genuine warmth touched me; I saw none of the detachment or skepticism common among American teens, none of the need to be "cool" around adults.

When the first reel of the movie had finished, there was an intermission to set up the next one. A group of teens stood up and came to the front, prompting applause from the crowd. I watched them as they began to perform a skit of some kind. As the skit was in Portuguese, I turned to Roberto, who tried to translate and explain what I was watching. I could barely hear what he was saying over the roar of the crowd. Evidently they were enacting a story having to do with HIV/AIDS education outreach. The crowd was completely engaged, yelling answers to questions posed by the actors, cheering them on at certain points, and even hissing at something one of them said. I tried to follow along based upon the actions, noticing that one of the kids in the skit kept saying "UNICEF."

I asked Roberto about the UNICEF references once the skit had finished. He told me that the dialogue had gone as follows:

"If you think you might be sick, where do you go?"
"UNICEF."
"If you think your mother might be sick, where do you go?"
"UNICEF."
"What saved your mother's life?"
"UNICEF."
"What made your own life possible?"
"UNICEF."

I broke into tears, thinking how lucky I was, how privileged, to make even a small contribution to UNICEF's work of saving the lives of children.

After leaving the movie that night, I was agape at another constant feature of African life: bugs. We stayed at a guesthouse outside of Beira, and upon exiting a tiny restaurant nearby, we encountered hundreds, if not thousands, of huge, long-winged insects attracted to a lone streetlight, flying directly in the path we needed to follow. While everyone else in our group commented on the bugs and batted them away, I seemed to be the only one who was absolutely terrified. Not wishing to come off as ridiculous, I inhaled deeply, held my breath, and continued on my way, pretending nothing was wrong.

Later that night, I couldn't sleep. I lay in my bed in my sparsely furnished room, trying to decide if I should cover myself with the blanket so as to keep the legions of smaller bugs still buzzing by my ear off my body or leave the blanket off so I could stay cool. Before I could fix on a strategy, the power went out. The darkness was so complete that it felt suffocating, causing me to panic. I had my laptop with me, and as I still had some battery power left, I calmed myself by putting on a DVD to watch. Halfway through the program, I heard a noise coming from the window.

What was it—an animal? A snake? A huge insect? My heart stopped and I waited. Chip's room was down the hall, but the others from our group were sleeping in another building. Surprising myself with my boldness, I went over to the window and very slowly lifted the shade to find dozens of eyes staring back at me. I jumped in fright. Once I caught my breath, I realized that these people were local villagers who had been walking back to their huts when they had seen the faint purple glow from my computer peeking out from my room. They had come, wondering what it could be. They pointed at my computer, and I held it up for them to see. We all got a hearty laugh.

My visit with Rosa came two days into our meanderings in the country. "The first baby that lived," she had said. When I got over the shock of that softly spoken answer, I pulled the single metal chair in the room closer to her bed and sat down to talk. A member of the UNICEF Mozambique team joined us to interpret, while the rest of our group moved outside to talk with other women at the clinic.

"What's your baby's name?" I asked.

She gazed down at her newborn and caressed her cheek. "She has not yet been named." My Mozambique colleague explained that babies in this part of Africa do not get their names at birth, but rather several days later.

"How did you come to be in this clinic? Do you live nearby?"

She didn't understand my query, so I tried some other lines

of questioning to get at her birth story. I learned that she lived in a one-room mud hut located in a village four hours away by foot. When she went into labor, she had been working in a rice paddy, picking rice and placing it in the basket she carried. "Water up to here," she said, gesturing at her knees.

"So what did you do when labor began?"

"I put down my basket and began my walk here."

I couldn't believe it. "You walked in the hot sun for four hours while you were in labor?" It was over 106 degrees outside, making it difficult for me just to sit there.

She nodded as if there was nothing unusual about that.

"Was someone with you?"

She shook her head. "No."

"Did you bring anything with you to the clinic—clothes, baby things?"

Again she shook her head. I could see she found my questions odd.

For a second time in five minutes, I found myself at a loss. Looking at Rosa and her new baby, I couldn't help but register the huge disparity between Rosa's situation and my own first experience giving birth to our son Lee, at one of Long Island's finest hospitals. I had prepped for that day for weeks. Lamaze classes. Every baby book I could get my hands on. Then a huge surprise baby shower, making sure I had every single thing I could imagine I'd need for our new arrival. My mother had bought me an overnight bag to take to the hospital. I had packed it over a month before my due date, filling it with a bottle of champagne, a list of phone numbers of friends and family (this was long before cell phones), a book I thought I'd actually have time to read, and a pretty nightgown I naively thought I would get to wear for the experience. The idea that something could go wrong never crossed my mind.

After more than twenty-four hours of labor, my doctors ordered a cesarean section, and with my husband Donald in the operating room holding my hand, they delivered a beautiful healthy boy. I cried. Donald cried. We popped the bottle and celebrated. Family and friends soon arrived, and we welcomed our new son in my flower-filled room.

And here was Rosa, who had walked for four hours, alone, in the heat. She didn't have a nursery, much less a cradle or bassinette. She didn't have doctors.

How could this be? It was difficult to get my mind around the disparities between our experiences. Why did I get to deliver my child in a modern, fully equipped hospital while Rosa lay alone in a small room that served as a ward, her only luxuries the screens in the window and the bed net over her head?

I had screamed for and received an epidural as soon as the pain of labor became unbearable. Rosa lacked even the most basic pain medication. I had been upset that my insurance only allowed me a sonogram every three months while pregnant; she probably didn't even realize sonograms existed. If Rosa had had any kind of birthing complication, both she and her child likely would have died; no one at the clinic was equipped or trained to provide anything more than basic assistance. Nor was there an ambulance outside to take her to a hospital for help, or a hospital anywhere near enough.

I stared at Rosa and tried to imagine what this day had been like for her. I had had no idea that birthing was like this for most women in developing nations. How could I have been so blind?

I felt a desperate urge to call my kids, to hear their voices and feel reassured they were okay. If I had been living in Mozambique, I might well have died giving birth to Lee.

And if I had been fortunate enough to survive the complications that had led to my cesarean, Lee almost certainly would not have. I found myself offering up a silent prayer of thanks as I watched Rosa hold her new baby.

As Rosa recounted still more details about her life, I didn't detect anger or suffering in her eyes so much as a deep soulfulness, an understanding of the tenuousness of life, an acceptance of its hardships. "My first baby was dead at birth, my second I lost early on." She gazed down at her sleeping baby, and joy shone on her face. "But yesterday was yesterday. Today is today. And today I have a daughter."

Once again, tears filled my eyes. "You do, and it's wonderful." I was deeply touched by her willingness to speak with me, and by the connection I felt with her, despite all that divided us. We were talking mother to mother. We both knew what it was like to hold a baby in our arms, to thank G-d that it was alive and healthy, and that it was ours.

But if I thought this was all to Rosa's story—if I thought I could even begin to conceive of what she had been through and would continue to go through—I was wrong. I reached out and touched her baby's tiny foot through the sheet. "She's beautiful."

The baby stirred but just as suddenly settled back down. "She is, but let's hope she is also strong."

"What do you mean?"

She adjusted the fabric that swaddled her sleeping child, lovingly stroking her chubby cheeks. "I have the AIDS virus. Since I found out I was pregnant, I came here to get the drugs to stay healthy." She nodded at her baby. "And to keep this one healthy."

Everything I had learned about UNICEF's efforts to combat HIV/AIDS had been so abstract. The AIDS outreach skit the evening before had made an impression, but it was only in talking to Rosa that I fully understood the difference aid organizations were making. This woman sitting across from me had a healthy baby because there was a UNICEF. Despite the hardships she faced, Rosa had been able to go to a clinic and get the anti-retroviral drugs she needed because of the generosity of donors in my country and elsewhere, and because people like my team at the U.S. Fund were working to raise awareness of the need. While I had been motivated before to work for my new organization, hearing this part of Rosa's story confirmed that by doing what I was doing in New York, I could really make a difference.

"How long will you stay here at the clinic?" I asked.

"Just tonight. I can't stay away from my husband. We do not stay away from our husbands."

I nodded in understanding. "And you will walk home?"

She nodded. "Of course."

"When will your baby see a doctor?"

She looked at me strangely. "The next day."

Now it was I who didn't understand.

She mouthed a slurry of words, which the interpreter translated. "I will come back every day. I need to, for the anti-retroviral drugs."

"And you will carry your baby?"

"I will carry my baby."

"Why can't you just take the drugs with you?"

She shook her head. "I don't know how to read. I can't understand the instructions. So I do what I can."

I was beside myself. This woman would need to walk four

hours each way under the hot sun for several weeks to obtain the drugs that would prevent her from transmitting the virus to her baby through her breast milk. Yet Rosa didn't think her walk was a hardship; it was normal to her, something women in her village had to do for the health of their children. This pointed to a deeper, underlying commonality between Rosa and me, and in fact, most women everywhere. When we become mothers, we are so overcome by the joy of parenthood that everything else fades into the background. Obstacles and hardships that might have stymied us before no longer seem so significant. We do what we have to do.

It was time to go—our group was waiting. I posed for a picture with Rosa, kissed her and her baby, and walked outside, where I would continue to speak to health-care workers about HIV/AIDS and where I would continue to learn.

Three days later, we returned to Maputo for a break and a day of meetings before heading back to the United States. It had been an extremely emotional first encounter with a developing country, and my mind was reeling. Yet one more unforgettable moment lay in store.

During our initial briefing, our staff had mentioned that Mozambique was a predominantly Christian country with a sizable Muslim minority. I had raised my hand and asked if any Jews resided there. The staff member giving the presentation responded, "Yes, we have Jews here." Somehow the way she said it sounded comical to me, as if Jews were prized possessions, not people. I asked if there were synagogues in Maputo and learned that indeed there was one. I wanted to see it.

I grew up in a Jewish home, celebrating the arrival of the Sabbath every Friday night by lighting candles with my family. I can still picture my mother standing in our dining room, apron tied at her waist, eyes closed, singing the Hebrew words, orange sunset shining through the glass doors that led from our dining room out onto our back patio. Standing almost five feet, nine inches tall, with beautiful blond hair tied perfectly in a French knot, sky blue eyes, and an easy smile, my mom invited us all to acknowledge this holy day of rest. Then my dad chanted, both over the wine in a silver wine cup that had belonged to my grandfather and over freshly baked challah. My brother and I knew he did this more for my mom than out of his own deep religious conviction, yet each week we ignored that fact and said "Amen" when he finished, digging into the dinner my mom put before us.

Memories such as this have left me with an immediate connection to other Jews, regardless of how different we might otherwise be. Perhaps this is why I find myself always seeking out the local congregation when I am far from home. On this day, the UNICEF Mozambique team had arranged for me to visit the Maputo synagogue. I was driven to what at one time must have been a beautiful white colonial building, framed by two large columns and featuring a large Star of David above the entrance. Walking inside, I found the place in disrepair. The wood pews and white walls seemed solid enough, but boxes and other objects were strewn about, and it didn't seem like much prayer was taking place.

A man greeted me and informed me that they did hold services in the building. Maputo had once had a thriving Jewish community of Europeans who had fled the Nazis.

During Mozambique's civil war, almost all the Jews left, most going to South Africa. The building was requisitioned for use as a munitions storage facility. When the war ended, the authorities returned it to the remaining members of the Jewish community. They had worked on making repairs, yet much remained to be done, as evidenced by the gaping holes I now noticed in the walls.

I asked questions about the Jewish community. Did Jews all live in the same area? Did anyone maintain a kosher home? Were regular weekly Sabbath prayer services held? How large was the community?

The answer to this last question took me by surprise. I had expected to hear that Jews represented only a small percentage of the city's population, but was shocked to learn that they numbered exactly seven souls.

"What's it like, having such a small community?" I asked. Jewish tradition holds that a community needs ten adult men (although in reform congregations, women can now fulfill these roles as well) to hold a prayer service, and Maputo didn't even have that many.

"You think that's bad," my new friend said, grinning. "Some of us don't talk to the rest of us, so instead of one service, we have two!"

I couldn't help but laugh. Such divisions were so typical, not just of Judaism but of other religions as well. I had often heard a joke told in the Jewish community where I grew up: "If you ask four Jews, you'll get five opinions." Here in Maputo, that had certainly been proven true.

Despite the sadness I felt at the dwindling of this once-proud community, I also felt a sense of comfort just being in this building. All along on this trip, I had been pushed headlong into unfamiliarity. The sheer level of poverty and Rosa's story of hardship had been hard to process. At this synagogue, I felt strangely and unexpectedly at home, as I might have felt in any other city in the world upon finding a synagogue. I hadn't considered that in a country as distant in every respect from my own there would be Jews. But what do you know, here there were seven.

Back in New York, I returned to my normal life. Yet things had changed for me. Thanks especially to my visit with Rosa, I had fallen headfirst into a love affair with both Africa and UNICEF. I didn't just want to stay with the U.S. Fund and become CEO; now I *had* to become CEO. I knew I needed to continue to stretch myself, to take that extra step and face my fears, whatever they were, so as to earn the right to take the helm of this organization. For the rest of the winter of 2007, I focused on winning the CEO job. I knew I needed to investigate other professional opportunities in case I did not get it, but I couldn't bring myself to do it. I didn't want other opportunities. I wanted *this* one.

By April, the competition for CEO was down to myself and three other people. As a final part of the interview process, the search committee asked us each to do a presentation explaining what UNICEF did. Recognizing that some on the board were concerned about my lack of experience, I took this opportunity to tell them about what I had seen in Mozambique and the people I had met. "Here's what the reports say about Mozambique," I told them, "but here's the reality that I encountered with my own two eyes. I met a woman named Rosa"—and the story flowed out of me.

Several weeks later, I heard that I had gotten the job. I knew then—and I still know—that this never would have happened had I not visited Mozambique. Rosa in particular was my inspiration. If she could give birth with so little and fight so hard to ensure that her child is free from AIDS, then there had to be more I could do to help. I wanted to travel to other new places that would challenge me and shift my perspective. I suddenly saw my age of fifty as an ideal time to start fresh and approach the world again with childlike curiosity.

As of this writing, some five years after my visit, the situation in Mozambique remains dire. The economy has continued to grow at a steady pace, but 54 percent of the country's people still live in poverty, and fewer than half of all households have access to clean drinking water. Unacceptably high numbers of mothers and children still die of preventable causes, although the country has passed legislation designed to protect all children and created a national council to protect especially vulnerable children. HIV/AIDS remains among the highest causes of child deaths as well as of children's increased vulnerability to poverty and deprivation (since their parents and other caregivers are getting sick). The country's first national survey on HIV/AIDS, performed in 2009, found that over 10 percent of men and women are still HIV-positive. The country continues to count almost 2 million orphans, a quarter of whom lost their parents to AIDS.[4]

The responses and assistance continue. A host of aid organizations work hard to get residents of Mozambique the care they need, relying on new and different innovations as they become available. In places where the population lacks ready access to HIV testing, nutritional counseling, information about prevention, or other basic health services, community leaders with basic health-care training come together to serve as a warning system for emerging problems and ensure that their communities are aware of preventative measures such as immunization. Community theater groups continue to serve as health educators, performing skits like the one I saw, informing and engaging those whose lack of literacy or media access has cut them off from potentially life-saving information.

UNICEF and other groups have also been designating and training individuals as community health workers, giving them kits with basic medicines to treat rampant sicknesses like diarrhea, malaria, and pneumonia. HIV activists—often people who themselves are suffering from AIDS—provide social support, coaching people on how to take ARV medicines and following up to make sure they do take them. These initiatives are a far cry from the high-tech solutions available in countries like the United States, but in the absence of more trained doctors and nurses and more sophisticated interventions, they're saving lives.[5]

I never saw Rosa again, never heard what happened to her and her daughter. Yet I remain grateful for the privilege of meeting her. I see life differently, appreciating that many things I had previously taken for granted are not necessities, but luxuries. Equally important, she helped me to understand that regardless of our economic differences, I could no longer see myself as fundamentally different from people living half a world away, under very different circumstances. The material divide may be huge, but we are all human beings with the same goals and desires. We all love our children and want the best for them. This is the same whether we walk four hours to give birth, or drive, as I did, for less than ten minutes. It might sound trite, but it's absolutely true and often forgotten: what joins us as human beings is at least as important as what divides us.

2. WITNESSING DARFUR

Sudan, Fall 2007

You gain strength, courage, and confidence
by every experience in which you really stop
and look fear in the face.

—ELEANOR ROOSEVELT

I HAVE A PICTURE in my mind that stays with me wherever I go. A little girl stands on a dock, holding the hand of a little boy who is her brother. The girl is six years old, the boy four. They are about to board a ship bound for a land they have never visited and only vaguely heard of—a faraway land whose inhabitants speak a strange language. The children have only learned a few days earlier that they will be traveling, and that they will do so without either of their parents.

The year is 1939, and the ship is bound for the United States. The little girl is my mom, the boy my uncle. Their parents have arranged their departure hoping to spare them from the horrors the Nazis are already inflicting on the Jews in Vienna, Austria. My grandparents have arranged for a woman they know to accompany my mother and uncle. The children do not know her—in fact, they are never told her first name and will never see her again after the voyage. This nameless woman saved their lives, and her legacy taught me from my earliest moments of understanding that one person can indeed make a difference.

A picture of another ship also looms large for me—one my maternal grandfather boarded in 1939. This ship, the SS *St. Louis,* left Europe bound for Cuba in what is often referred to as the Voyage of the Damned. My grandfather planned to settle in that island nation, send for his family, and start life anew. Yet when the boat entered Havana's harbor, Cuban authorities boarded and informed the passengers (mostly Jews) that their documents were fraudulent and they could not enter the country.

The boat languished in the harbor for forty days while the world debated the fate of its passengers. No country would agree to accept the refugees, not even the United States. The ship was forced to return to Europe, where most of its passengers perished at the hands of the Nazis. My grandfather was one of the few who survived, and I had the privilege of hearing his story firsthand, teaching me just what happens when the world turns its back, ignores the facts, and allows innocent people to die.

These two pictures together have inspired me never to sit on the sidelines. I am committed to using any tools and whatever power I might possess to fight for justice and compassion, and to keep on fighting even when exhaustion sets in. Thanks to my family legacy, I know that when I choose to be the person who makes a difference—when I care, when I act, when I give—my life is at its richest.

I thought often of my mother and grandfather during the spring and summer of 2007 as the humanitarian disaster in

Darfur continued to unfold before the world. Fighting had erupted four years earlier in this region of Sudan between government forces and several rebel groups who had accused Sudan's Arab government of discriminating against non-Arab (Christian and animist) minorities. The fighting had gotten ugly by 2004, with pro-government militias conducting what the United Nations termed a scorched-earth campaign against Darfur's black African population, destroying numerous villages, forcing hundreds of thousands of people from their homes, and creating one of the world's worst humanitarian crises.

The global community was slow to respond on legal grounds; because the conflict had not been declared a genocide or a threat to neighboring countries, international law forbade foreign countries from intervening without the government's consent. The only outside force on the ground was a peacekeeping force deployed by the African Union and the UN, yet this force was small and unable to stop combatants, especially the pro-government militias, from razing villages, raping and pillaging, and committing other atrocities against civilians.

By 2006, the violence in Darfur had affected some 4 million people, half of them children. As atrocities continued and casualties mounted (one report estimated that more than 450,000 people had likely died), the UN drew up plans to send in a more substantial peacekeeping force. The warring parties signed a peace agreement, arousing a flicker of hope, but violence only increased after the treaty was signed, and the president of Sudan soon vowed publicly to keep the UN peacekeepers from entering his country. As the situation continued to deteriorate, rallies were held in the United States and celebrities began to involve themselves, drawing the

American public's attention. In the spring of 2007, President George W. Bush imposed sanctions against Sudan's government. While many groups were providing assistance to the people of the region, acts of violence against aid workers forced some groups to pull out. Even the international aid group Oxfam had to leave a large camp for internally displaced persons in Sudan for safety reasons.[1]

I had been reading about events in Darfur and had been appalled at what I was learning. Aware of how the world had failed to respond to Nazi aggression against the Jews until it was too late, and how some people continued to deny the reality of the Holocaust, I refused to sit back and pretend events in Darfur were not happening.

I felt a strong urge to bear witness, to see it for myself. I remember as a child asking my mom how the world could have allowed Nazis to kill Jews, especially Jewish children. I couldn't fathom how good people had failed to speak out and do something. And yet, here I was, doing nothing while children in Darfur perished. In my heart, I knew that if I was to be true to myself, my family, and my heritage, I needed to go to Darfur and use what I learned there to capture the attention of as many people as possible.

In September 2007, an opportunity finally presented itself. I met with supermodel Dayle Haddon to explore ways in which she might help UNICEF, and she asked if I'd be willing to accompany her to Darfur. I knew when I joined the U.S. Fund for UNICEF that the organization had a long history of working with famous people—movie stars, models, athletes, world leaders, business magnates—to promote the needs of the world's children. In fact, UNICEF was the first organization to have celebrity ambassadors, starting with Audrey Hepburn and Danny Kaye. Since joining the U.S. Fund,

I had often found myself in conversations with famous individuals, struggling to appear nonchalant while the child inside me was jumping up and down yelling, "I can't believe I'm standing next to this person!"

In Dayle's case, I had come to the meeting with a bit of trepidation. I am always self-conscious and very aware of my size when forced to stand next to women who are a perfect size two. It's more than just size: most celebrities know how to stand, where to look, what to wear, and how best to show it off. This leaves me feeling somewhat like their older aunt who has been squeezed into the family photograph. Fortunately, Dayle put me entirely at ease. She is not merely gorgeous but intelligent, well spoken, and sincere. She possessed a strong desire to work with us on behalf of the world's children, and she was frustrated that we hadn't yet found a suitable role she could play. She arrived at our meeting prepared, revealing a strong knowledge of children's issues. We immediately bonded as women, talking about our kids and the challenges and thrills of being working moms.

I was excited about the idea of visiting Darfur with Dayle, but later that evening, as I sat at dinner and told my husband and kids about the trip, I felt a wave of fear. My experience in Mozambique had introduced me to grinding poverty, but it hadn't posed any real security issues. Darfur was seeing active combat; even aid workers were being targeted. Was it safe to go? Was I up for the challenge?

Ultimately, I decided that I was. People were still arguing about whether the conflict in Darfur was genocide or "merely" a civil war, but whatever the case, it was a humanitarian disaster. Large numbers of innocent civilians were suffering, and many individuals and governments around the world were sitting by and doing nothing. I was not going to be one of them. Even if it meant taking a personal risk, I needed to use my platform as CEO of the U.S. Fund to stand up and say, "The disaster here is real. I've seen it with my own eyes. And it needs to end."

As I began to investigate putting the trip together, Dayle was arranging for us to report on our experiences afterward at a meeting of the Women's Forum for the Economy and Society (a group made up of influential women from around the world) scheduled to take place in Deauville, France. This would be a powerful opportunity to raise awareness and do our part for the people of Darfur. I reminded her that we still didn't know if the United Nations would sanction our trip, given the precarious security situation. Nonetheless, we made plans to leave just a few weeks later, in early October, with the understanding that up until the day we went, the trip could be canceled at any time for security reasons.

When I leave on a trip, it usually isn't such a big deal for my kids; they're used to my frequent travel. This time, it was. My sons Lee and James had heard a lot about Darfur on the news, and they knew that this was not just another trip. Lee, twelve years old at the time, was especially emotional. The morning I left, he gave me an extra-strong hug and said, "Mom, are you sure this trip is okay?" He didn't say, "I don't want you to go," and frankly, I'm not sure what I would have done if he had said that.

"I'll call you when I get there," I said. "And you can tell me your one thing from the day."

We have a ritual in our family: When I travel, each of my kids needs to think of one important thing from their day to tell me. We do this for two reasons. First, because I want to keep current on important things happening in my kids' lives, but also because my kids often do not understand that it isn't always possible for me to have long, rambling conversations with everyone. They forget that I am calling from a remote location in the desert and have been known to eat up five minutes of a call arguing with one another while I am trying to get them to talk to me! Having them think of an important thing to tell me forces them to plan for my call and be ready to share. Sometimes just hearing one another's voices is enough, but this time, given our mutual concerns, I intended to call a bit more often than usual, hopefully giving us all a feeling that I was safe and so were they.

To get to Khartoum, Sudan's capital city, we had to change planes in Europe. The trip was excruciatingly long, and to make matters worse, I was unable to sleep on account of nerves. Before we left New York, I had taken a required UN security course intended to prepare me for things like what to do when insurgents attack your jeep, how to spot a roadside bomb, and how to shake out your bedding to avoid scorpions. The day before we left, we had received an alert saying that the security situation had become so dangerous that we might be denied entrance to the camps upon our arrival, for our own safety. Dayle and I contemplated not going, but in the end we proceeded, hoping for the best but not knowing what awaited us.

Dayle helped distract me from my own worries in her unique way. When we first boarded the plane, she was her gorgeous self, dressed ethereally in a wafty linen dress and scarf (I, by contrast, was sweating up a storm in jeans and a huge T-shirt). We found our seats, and while I got settled, she took out a small bottle and sprayed her seat. "Got to make sure it's clean," she said as I caught her eye.

She continued her ritual, taking out a handheld device that looked like a calculator and running it over the seat. "This is a sonic device that is supposed to kill germs." Next, she swallowed a pill that boosted her immune system. "I do this because I travel a lot, and I don't like to take any chances. It's important to do your research and take care of yourself. I work out a lot before going on trips like this, too."

I totally understood, and when she asked if I'd like her to spray my seat and go over it with the sonic device, I accepted. Far easier to worry about germs than to worry about Darfur.

We landed in Khartoum late in the evening and were met by UNICEF staffers. The airport, which smelled of a mixture of spices, urine, and petrol, was crowded with people. The atmosphere was tense; rebels had apparently attacked nearby in recent days. Shouting broke out as travelers ran around looking for their bags. We saw devout Muslims praying on small rugs as well as women covered head to toe despite the heat, as was Muslim custom. We were so exhausted that we practically sleepwalked over to the car, and although the driver pointed out sights along the way, we nodded off, barely hearing a word. We did register that it was Ramadan and all restaurants were closed during the daytime. If we wanted to eat, we would have to get up before sunrise. We made plans to do that, checked into our rooms, and fell into bed.

Hours later, a noise startled me awake. I had no idea at first what it was, but then I recognized it as the Muslim call to prayer. I opened the wooden shutters that covered my window to find the sun just starting to rise, casting orange and rose-colored light on the angular stone buildings and walls of ancient Khartoum.

In a nearby courtyard, men were assembling with their prayer mats and offering morning prayers. Years earlier, I had traveled to another ancient city, Jerusalem. I had arrived at night in Tel Aviv, slept during the car ride to the Holy City, and checked into a hotel with wooden shutters. In the morning, just as now, I had opened those shutters to the faithful going to prayer—only those were Jews at the Wailing Wall. Now I reflected on how delightfully similar Islam and Judaism are, despite being so often at odds. As an American Jew, I felt surprised and reassured to find something so familiar in a place that I had mistakenly assumed would feel foreign.

Dayle and I had a quick breakfast and went to the UNICEF office for a briefing, just as my group had done in Mozambique. The office was housed behind barbed wire in the middle of Khartoum. We learned that the situation in Darfur had calmed somewhat but was still tense; we would be able to drive by a camp for internally displaced people, but it would still be too dangerous to enter. Darfur was in level 3 security, which meant essential UNICEF personnel were allowed to remain, but not their families. (Level 4 was a total withdrawal from the country.) We were warned to keep a low profile at all times and not photograph strategic structures such as bridges or official buildings; security personnel might take us as a threat, kidnapping or attacking us; this had happened to other Westerners.

We planned to fly from Khartoum to Darfur, where UN jeeps would meet us at the airport to drive us by the camp. Before we could depart, we had to obtain special UN travel passes. While we waited for these documents, Dayle and I strolled around downtown Khartoum, walking through dusty streets filled with old carts and what looked like even older cars and spotting the Nile, a beautiful, meandering river that transported us back into history. Entering the market, we passed through narrow streets and alleyways and stopped at a rickety little table where Dayle bought a carved wooden crocodile for her grandchildren. At a nearby dress shop, I tried on several *abayas*—Islamic robes worn by women.

All along, the Arabic I was hearing sounded so close to the Hebrew I had learned when I was a kid; I could even follow some of the conversations around me. Everything about this place felt comfortable (with the exception of our heightened security fears). The modesty with which Muslim women cover their heads reminded me of the wigs and hats I had seen on religious Jewish women my entire life. The rules governing dietary restrictions were akin to those that dictate what is kosher and what is not. I couldn't help but wonder if Jews like me were culturally more similar to our Arab brothers and sisters than we were to our Christian siblings.

We boarded an old UN propeller plane with a member of our Sudan staff. I hadn't met anyone from the staff before, so I did my best to appear brave and completely professional, trying to hide the fact that I don't like old propeller planes. Even though the ride was much smoother than I had expected, my fear was obvious and we were all laughing about it by the time we arrived.

You could see the camps from the air, stretching out a long distance, surrounded by sand. Upon landing in Al Fashir, a large town in Darfur, we were met by Dr. Haydar Nasser, an

Iraqi doctor who ran the local UNICEF office. Nasser was handsome, with dark skin, a small mustache, and a bit of a five o'clock shadow. Dayle and I were immediately impressed, finding him knowledgeable, calm, and reliable—clearly a man of deep inner strength. Having lived in Darfur for some time, he understood the local culture and customs as well as the political situation. "Whatever you do," he counseled, "don't promise anything to people you will meet. Because we on the ground will be called upon to deliver."

We drove to the local UNICEF office for a security briefing. The squat concrete building seemed like a fortress; in addition to barbed wire, huge tires had been placed in front of the building and half buried in the sand so as to block carborne attacks. Members of our security team again told us not to travel alone, and they warned that we might have to leave unexpectedly because of the volatile security situation. Although we were only going to be driving near the camps for the day, we had to stay in constant contact with our guards. Dayle, Dr. Nasser, and I would travel in the middle of a three-jeep convoy. We would receive regular alerts from the first jeep. If they failed to ping us, we were to turn around immediately.

With that we were off, driving fast past dusty stone buildings and a huge UN complex. Al Fashir was more primitive than Khartoum. The open markets we passed seemed to be selling everything, from shoes to unrecognizable parts of animal carcasses, the stalls run by female vendors bundled in black from head to toe. Camels strutted by, some ridden by brightly dressed women carrying babies. We passed wheelbarrows filled with oranges, some ripe, some not, trucks belonging to other nongovernmental organizations, and a few mosques with minarets. On a number of corners, signs

depicting a gun with a red X marked over it reminded us
that war and lawlessness were a fact of life here.

Other sights seemed equally exotic. Staring out the windows, we saw charcoal-skinned men standing on street corners, wearing squarish hats and long, sparkling white tunics.
The doors were painted a striking blue, set off nicely, Dayle
thought, from the walls of gray and brown stone. The streets
were little more than dirt roads, and garbage was strewn
about freely. We passed buses so jammed with people we
thought they'd topple over. And then there was the parking
lot for camels. Villagers apparently rode their camels into
town and left them tied to stakes in the ground, while going
about their business. Each of the thirty to forty camels looked
identical to me—how could people tell which one was theirs?
Did you have to pay to leave your camel there? Our guard
made a joke about "camel lot/Camelot," and we all giggled
nervously.

Leaving Al Fashir, we drove into the desert and continued
for hours. The earth here was a reddish clay color, and low-
slung mountains rose up in the distance beneath a heavy blue-
gray sky. It was about 110 degrees outside; when we drank
from our plastic bottles, we found the water was not warm,
but hot. As one of the members of the UNICEF Sudan staff
had said, living here had convinced him there was some truth
to the idea that "the sun was so hot that you could fry an egg
on a car." Dayle remarked that you had to be very calm, almost zenlike, just to function in such an environment.

We passed scattered scrub bushes, dying or barren trees,
villages of wooden lean-to huts, and women wrapped in
bright Arabian-looking robes and *abayas*. Then there were

vast stretches of nothing, just desert. Periodically, we would hear "slow down, slow down" over the walkie-talkies; we needed to keep a certain distance behind the jeep in front of us so that we would be in a position to escape and get help if they were attacked. We occasionally saw soldiers in camouflage carrying heavy weapons. The road drifted in and out, sometimes becoming little more than hard-packed sand. Our driver told us stories of sand storms, swirling earth so thick you could not see. We stared out the windows for long periods without talking, just soaking it all in.

Some time later, in the middle of nowhere, we approached a small cement house by the side of the road that served as a government checkpoint. The tension in our car immediately ratcheted up. "Okay, cameras down, sunglasses off," our security guard told us. "Remember, no eye contact." Soldiers ventured out to speak to our driver, serious and unsmiling, weapons slung over their shoulders. I was terrified, as I had heard reports of people being shot at checkpoints. What made it worse was seeing how young these soldiers were—little more than boys manning these big machine guns. There were no witnesses; they could shoot us and nobody would know what happened. I kept my head down and avoided eye contact, as we had been instructed.

I couldn't understand a word of what the soldiers and our driver were saying. Time seemed to stop and I thought of a time just after Palestinian leader Yasser Arafat died when my work with the Anti-Defamation League left me sitting on a bus in Jordan with other American Jews. We were parked outside a Jordanian government compound in Amman, Jordan's capital city, waiting to be cleared to go inside to meet with Arafat's successor, Mahmoud Abbas. Intellectually I knew I was safe there; we were guests of the government.

But recent events in the region had left me very nervous. I couldn't help but think that our bus could blow up at any second, and I wondered how actual victims of bombings had felt moments before it happened. Had they had a premonition? Did they know they were in trouble?

As the soldiers continued to question our driver, my mind drifted further to a story my mother had told me years ago. When she was a very young girl in Vienna, the Nazi soldiers had terrified her. One night they came for her father, and he was forced to hide in the hall closet to avoid being taken. My mother had to answer the door and lie, saying her father wasn't there and she didn't know where he was. She told me she had been so scared that she would screw it up and he would be discovered. She felt powerless in the face of their assumed absolute power. I now was in a similar situation, lacking all control over my destiny. One false move, I thought, could cost us our lives. I stayed calm, and fortunately, a few moments later, the soldiers waved us through.

An hour or two later, we neared the IDP camp. "We cannot visit in the camps," our security guard said, "but we will drive very fast as a security precaution around the perimeter, then drive quickly inside." As we raced across the desert toward the camps, kicking up dust, we saw a huge tent city stretched out, home to tens of thousands of people. This was the second largest of these camps, and it had become so established that some residents had constructed thatched-roof huts in an attempt to replicate the homes they had lost when their villages had been attacked. As Dr. Nasser told us, the number of people living here had drained the area resources so much that friction had arisen between the town outside of the camp, Al Fashir, and the internally displaced people living in the camp. Camp residents had to roam farther and farther out of the camp in search of firewood, food, and work, thus making the women vulnerable to rape and the men vulnerable to murder.

We rolled down the windows to get a better look, and as we pulled onto the main road going through the camp, we were accosted by an almost indescribable stench—filth, garbage, or as Dayle put it, the smell of death. It was overwhelming. I saw primitive huts where women cooked over open fires, tents and shelters made of plastic stretched across poles, and even a few buildings made of mud brick. The school was an actual cement building with a cement floor; it seemed that these people weren't going home any time soon.

As we continued our drive-through, we heard the sound of singing. "Can't we stop just for a moment?" Dayle asked. "It seems safe enough." Our guard and driver consulted with their colleagues over the walkie-talkie, and to our surprise, they agreed. We got out and came upon a class for girls (the genders were segregated according to local custom) sitting on a dirt floor in a classroom with walls made of sticks. We met the teacher, and she had the children sing for us. The sounds of their voices and the white scarves around their heads seemed angelic. I found it breathtaking to witness normal life in some small way continuing in the camp.

Now that we were stopped in the camp, it seemed safe to proceed with more of a visit. The place reeked of smoke from cooking fires that the women had made in front of their huts. The people were beautiful—dark skin, almond eyes, strong cheekbones, handsome faces. We walked into a health clinic made of thatched bamboo and watched healthcare workers measuring the size of babies' arms to test for malnutrition. At a well, small children of perhaps five or six years of age were pumping precious water to carry back to their mothers, working hard under the hot sun.

I had heard about UNICEF's efforts to help people in the camps, and it was inspiring to see this firsthand. In addition to mobile health clinics like the one we visited, efforts on the ground included feeding centers, emergency shelter, sanitary facilities, and access to clean water. Schools and child-friendly spaces in the camp were created in an effort to give children who had fled their villages a sense of normalcy amidst the upheaval. Community health volunteers were deployed to educate camp dwellers about hygiene, since many internally displaced people came from rural areas and were not used to living among people packed densely together. UNICEF also provided counselors and other psychosocial care in an effort to help individuals struggling with the emotional aftermath of rape, killings, or other trauma.

We visited a school for boys and also one of the designated child-friendly spaces, enclosed by walls made of plastic and netting. Here I confirmed for myself that kids are in fact still kids, even in the most desperate and unhappy of places. At the child-friendly space, Dayle and I sat on the ground to play patty-cake and other games; the children crawled all over us and hugged us, thrilled to see us. Some touched our skin, intrigued by how white we were. Dayle took a small bottle of soap bubbles out of her purse and began to blow bubbles. The children were delighted, having never seen anything like it. She also took off her scarf to use as a jump rope, engaging a group of four- and five-year-olds in the game. The children sang for us and showed us pictures they were drawing. None of them spoke English, so we relied on our smiles and occasionally staff persons' translations to smooth the way. It is amazing how an outstretched hand can offset a difference in language. For a moment, I almost forgot where I was. I might as well have been back at a village in Mozambique or, for that matter, at a rural preschool in the United States.

The adults in the camp were different: they had been through hell, and it showed. At one point, we stopped in an open space to talk with some of the women. They spoke of recent events with ghostlike eyes, describing the day their village had been burned to the ground, as if they could still feel the flames or smell the acrid odor of torched belongings. Several described having been violated by their attackers, speaking in a vague, almost detached way, their omissions of details conveying just how raw the experiences still were for them. The worst stories involved children—mothers telling us how helpless they felt watching their sisters or daughters being raped.

One thirteen- or fourteen-year-old girl sat among us, silently at first. Judging from her size, she seemed much younger, a child rather than a woman. Then she spoke. Staring into the distance, in a voice just barely above a whisper, she described her last day in her village. She had risen at dawn to fetch water for her family. When she had returned, she had found rebels wreaking havoc. Tears ran down her face as she described finding her father and brothers dead, her mother and sisters cowering and crying. Then the men were upon her. First as a group, groping at her body, then taking turns raping her while the other rebels looked on and cheered, and while her mother and sisters hid their eyes with their hands and silently prayed. As she spoke, her eyes glazed over, as if she was removing herself from the scene she was describing, so great was the pain. That day, she, too, had died. She still breathed, she still functioned, she still cared for her younger sisters, but she wasn't the same.

Each person who spoke had a similar tale to tell. As they described it, the violence had all happened so quickly and yet seemed to last forever. There was sheer panic and frenzy—people screaming and crying and fleeing in every direction. Another woman reported that she had lost sight of her children and believed that all five had all been killed. Happily, she had found them alive and well inside the camp. The joy on her face was palpable, yet it contrasted starkly with the suffering of almost all the others around her. The women told us that they were just existing in the camp, not living. All their time and energy was devoted to securing their daily needs. It was dangerous to venture outside the camp for firewood and other supplies, but the women did so because they had no choice: the men would be killed if intercepted by hostile forces outside the camp; the women would "only" be raped. It was almost too much for me to take in. Making choices each day between rape and murder?

As the day progressed, I noted an unfortunate difference between the men and the women in the camp. The men walked around listlessly in their long white gowns and head scarves, appearing to lack anything to do. They were utterly devastated and emasculated. By contrast, the women were busy everywhere we went—fetching water, collecting firewood, cooking, watching children, digging makeshift latrines, even making bricks. Although they, too, had seen and felt the horrors of war, they seemed to show an inner resilience, a sense that yes, life was bad, but what choice did you have but to carry on? Their pain seemed to have morphed into a steely resolve to find their way back to life. I asked our UNICEF colleagues about this, and they agreed that the men had fallen victim not only to the horrors described by the women but to the depression that came with failing to meet cultural expectations. In their culture, men were supposed to provide and protect for their families. They had failed to do so, and now they stood riveted in place by shame.

We took many pictures that day in an effort to capture the desperation we were seeing. Images of skinny, malnourished children carrying plastic jugs of water on their heads and signs reading "No water. No life" remind me today just how scarce adequate nutrition, health care, and clean water are in a camp for displaced people. Other images remind me of how rickety and inadequate their huts were; I saw entire families squatting in squalor. And filth—dirt everywhere, in every picture, showing that basic sanitation was hard to come by. I caught people washing their hands in gray-colored water that had either been carried over long distances or pumped from a well and reused many times. I captured far too many images of young people seemingly just milling around. There were schools in the camp, but they were overcrowded and lacking in supplies. Hundreds, if not thousands, of children who should have been in school were not attending. Instead, they spent their time collecting wood, fetching water, and constructing huts for their families.

The saddest images I took showed the pain and trauma carved into the people's faces. With so many people crammed into such a small space, you could see in their eyes the fear of further violence. Clearly these people needed outside action to bring about a cessation of hostilities, so that they could go back to their villages and build new lives for themselves in peace. As I met and spoke with individual people, I locked eyes with them and passed along an unspoken promise: I would not forget them. I would use my voice to tell their stories and to get others to listen. And hopefully, one day soon, things would improve.

We finished our interviews with the women and headed back to the child-friendly space we had visited earlier. I was horrified at all I had heard, aching at their pain, and yet I also marveled at the tenacity of their spirit—the ability of these women to continue with their lives. As I walked through the camp, I tried to fit all this together in my brain, but I couldn't. I was lost in thought when my cell phone suddenly rang. It caught me offguard: here we were in an undeveloped part of Africa, and my reception was better than it often was in midtown Manhattan. I saw a familiar number on my screen; it was Lee, back home in New York City. "Mom, I'm having trouble with my math homework. Will you help me with it?"

It was surreal venturing through the camp, passing women cooking and children running barefoot, contending with the body odors and the smells that came from the latrines— while also figuring out algebra with my son, and afterward, an English assignment. But that's exactly what I did. My eyes fixed on my immediate surroundings while internally I was back at my kitchen counter, sitting next to Lee and peering over his shoulder. I couldn't help but compare the extreme differences between these two places. I sat on the ground to finish our conversation, and a little boy climbed onto my lap. I hugged him as I talked with Lee and wondered, as Lee hung up, whether my son would have the skills to cope if he ever found himself in a place like Darfur. For that matter, would I?

As we prepared to leave, a slight, elderly woman wearing an orange head scarf motioned to me and pulled me close, wanting to whisper something. I couldn't tell exactly how old she was, but she was hunched and missing her teeth, so I judged her clearly past middle age. Her knuckles were gnarled, and she was obviously malnourished, her spindly arms sticking out from her shawl. She took my hand and held it to her sunken cheek. Then, looking right at me, she kissed it. "Thank you," she said in perfect English. "Thank you. When you get home, you tell the Americans we know they are saving our lives." My eyes filled with tears upon hearing this, but then she said something else that *really* made me cry. "And we know the people of Abraham are helping us."

We stood there and gazed into each other's eyes, a Muslim woman who had lost everything, thanking an American Jew who would return to more than the other woman could ever imagine. We both knew it wasn't just Jews who were trying to help the people of Darfur—not by a long shot—but I had come here out of a sense of duty deriving from my Jewish roots, and this woman had somehow looked at me and been able to discern that. Her message ran through me. I felt it in my fingertips, in my toes, and in my heart.

Pulling myself together, I tried to convey to her what her statement meant to me "Thank *you*," I said. "Thank you for seeing the aid that is being offered and for finding the grace to offer gratitude. But, you do not owe me gratitude. Not at all. It is we who should be apologizing to you. It is our guilt and our shame to bear that we have left you here, forgotten, to suffer."

I had not put her here, and yet the reality was that I was free and she was not. I would return to riches and she would not. I didn't want or need to be thanked. I didn't want this woman, or any of the people of Darfur, to feel beholden to anyone for the help they were receiving. I remember once reading a series of interviews with "righteous gentiles"—Christian people who had put their and their families' lives at risk by hiding and protecting Jews during the Holocaust. Each interviewee had given the same answer when asked why he or she chose to act. It was hard to understand why the question was even being posed. "I did not choose," these people replied. "There was no choice to make. It was the right thing to do, the only thing to do." Standing in the desert with this woman, I fully understood their response. Being able to bestow help was a privilege, not a choice.

We don't get to choose the circumstances of our birth. Surely no one would choose poverty or encampment or brutality. So why do so many of us close our eyes and blindly continue with our everyday lives when people are suffering? Haven't we evolved enough to feel empathy and behave compassionately in the world? Why do we still reside in a world where the murder of innocent civilians, implicitly countenanced by global powers, still happens?

Today, some five years later, I continue to feel ashamed when thanked by grateful recipients of aid—ashamed that they have been left to suffer in the first place, and that I am in some small way complicit. My role as CEO of the U.S. Fund for UNICEF is far from self-sacrificial. I am not at risk, nor do I sacrifice my safety or my comfort each day. I look at UNICEF staffers who every day serve the poor, risking disease and violent attacks, spending time away from their families, and I find myself in awe of their efforts. I also find myself asking, "Am I doing enough?"

It was difficult leaving the camp—difficult saying good-bye to the people I had met. I stared out the back window of our jeep until the camp was no longer in sight. The road we were on was dangerous; it had recently been cleared by the UN for driving. In truth, it wasn't a road, but little more than two tracks in the sand continuing for hours. As we came to the first checkpoint, I was so lost in my thoughts that I almost forgot what I had been taught, only catching myself at the last minute and forcing my eyes to look down.

We traveled for several hours, finally arriving at a nearby village designated by UNICEF as a child-friendly village—a community that has worked with UNICEF to put their children first. After our jeeps were parked, Dayle and I and Dr. Nasser toured the village. Local residents approached Dr. Nasser seeking medical care and articulating the needs of the village. Dr. Nasser moved us with his compassion, the gentleness with which he examined a young girl and listened to her symptoms. The kids here were extremely excited to see visitors, since few came to such a remote location. Dayle spotted a class of boys sitting under a tree before a blackboard. "If you could have anything you wanted, what would it be?" she asked.

"A real school with real walls!" exclaimed a little boy.

The boys also wrote up little notes of greetings in English. "Thank you very muck for your efforts," read one of them, the imperfect spelling only deepening the authenticity of the sentiment.

Continuing along, we spotted sixty to seventy women

sitting quietly on the desert sand with their arms crossed. Clothed in long, flowing, brightly colored dresses, their heads covered, they were a picture of beauty but also one of extreme strength. It seemed obvious that these women were awaiting our arrival and equally obvious that they were on a mission of some sort. As we approached them, they greeted us and invited us to sit with them under a shady tree and hear of a problem they hoped to solve with our help.

Through an interpreter, a somewhat regal woman stood and related that their need for water forced them to work a heavy and tiring water pump, sometimes for hours on end. Her voice was initially hesitant, but it grew stronger as she clenched her fist and explained how this was impacting their children. "We work with our babies strapped on our backs," she said.

Another woman standing next to her added, "The constant movement is hurting our babies. We must find a way to save them from this."

Now the group was abuzz, telling stories of injuries to their children, describing how they had come together to solve the problem. These women had arrived at a novel idea for Africa: they would build a women's center where a couple of women could watch all the village's children while the rest took turns at the water pump.

The women had asked several nonprofits for financial support but had been turned down because other, competing priorities ranked higher. Although few of the women were literate or had any kind of formal education, they resolved to build a center themselves out of homemade bricks. "But who designed it?" I asked, thinking of my husband's many architect friends and the hours they spent working a design, determining measurements, honing their ideas.

"We did," said an older woman completely draped in a bright orange head scarf. She smiled, holding up her foot for me to see. "One brick is the size of my foot. We walked until we saw how big it was, and then we knew." Amazing— using their feet, they had walked off the building's footprint.

"But then who made the bricks, and where did the water come from?" asked Dayle.

The smiles of the women grew large as they reported having made the bricks themselves. To come up with the required water, each woman had agreed to forego a portion of her already meager allotment. The bricks were now done, and they wanted us to help them acquire the necessary cement.

These women were proud—you could see it in how straight they sat, how high they held their heads. They also took strength from one another. As we sat together, the conversation turned to all they had experienced in recent months. Their stories echoed what we had heard at the camp—rape, devastation, hunger. As one woman spoke, others reached out, placing hands on her arm as if to help her through her sentences, sharing her pain and offering her something to lean on. These outreached hands seemed to pull the bereaved back from the abyss, helping her come back to herself and focus on the future, not the past. Like the women at the camp, these women had made a choice not just to survive but to move forward. They were literally rebuilding themselves and their lives, holding on to the hope that tomorrow just might be a better day.

No way we were leaving without insuring that they would get their cement. Dayle agreed to pay for the cement out of her own pocket, and we made arrangements to have it delivered. As we drove away, I pondered an important lesson. We had arrived in Darfur with preconceived notions of what the people there would need or want. Yet these women knew their own needs and asked only that we help to satisfy them. We needed to respect those needs. This was not only about cultural sensitivity; it was about assumptions we'd made, assumptions that had failed to go to the source for information. I had to accept that for all my degrees and years of work experience, I and others like me do not have all the answers. We might bring suggestions, ideas, and tools, but only the expertise of those we are trying to help married with our own would bring about sustainable change.

I processed another lesson, too: the power of sisterhood, of being a woman who is part of a group of women. Watching these women in the village, I remembered the many moments I have turned to my own circle of women friends in times of trial. Somehow, through empathy, understanding, and commitment, we women become something greater when we come together. That's true no matter our geographic location or our economic status. Just as kids are kids the world over, so, too, are women everywhere the same.

We flew back to Khartoum and the next day began the long haul back to New York. To kill time on the airplane, I tried to put my thoughts down on paper, but I couldn't find the right words to describe the fear I had had before the trip, the horror of all I had heard about, or the level of hope I had encountered among the internally displaced people. How do you adequately describe conversations with children who have been raped and brutalized, yet who still believe that tomorrow will be a better day? I bit my tongue, keeping my emotions in check, as I made random, scattered notes and stared out the window. Later, when we landed, I felt so grateful for my home and for the life I had been given that I uttered a traditional Hebrew prayer, thanking G-d for protecting me and allowing me to reach this day.

When I got home, I put down my suitcase on our front porch, kicked off my shoes, and prepared as usual to make the mad dash to the laundry room to put my clothes in the washer. A few years earlier, I came back from a trip with bedbugs, and we had to professionally treat our whole house—every last piece of fabric and paper—to get rid of them. No way was that happening again. But before I could dash inside, something caught my eye. There on our front door, crayoned in big letters, was a sign reading, "Welcome Home, Mom." All the tears I had held back during the flight poured out as I ran into the house and hugged and kissed my husband and children.

When I had gotten into clean clothes and started the first round of laundry, I sat down to dinner and showed my family pictures from the trip. "Unbelievable," Donald said.

"They really are living like that?" Lee asked.

"Those are the lucky ones," I told him, "those who survived." Yet I had a haunting sense that the pictures couldn't begin to do justice to the reality in Darfur. They just couldn't convey the nauseating smells or the sun so hot that at times I felt like passing out.

"What are the kids like there?" Lee asked.

"Yeah, and what about school?" James chimed in. "Do they go? And do the people smile? Are they happy or sad?"

I handled their questions as best I could, keenly aware of the huge discrepancy between my normal life here in New York and life in Darfur—the chicken on my plate, two pieces, not just one; the shelter over my head, made of bricks, not sticks; the plush towels I had used when showering, while the people at the camp lacked a shower, much less towels.

"Did you bring us anything, Mom?" Lee asked.

Normally when I go overseas, I bring back souvenirs. This time, I had nothing, save a small vial of sand from the desert I'd stooped to collect. I pulled it out of my pocket and showed it to them. They put it on the shelf, next to carvings I'd brought them from Mozambique. Although the shelf has since filled in with objects from many more places, the vial of sand remains one of my favorite things there.

Over the next couple of weeks, as I tried to convey to friends what I had experienced, I found that many people didn't hear what I was trying to say. More than one person accused me of having become a "bleeding heart." I was not trying in any way to diminish, insult, or apologize for the lifestyle I had grown accustomed to. I have worked hard to get where I am, and so have most people in my circle. I just wondered if I truly needed it all—if, perhaps, less might suffice.

It took me a long time to process my trip. The following spring, as I prepared for our annual Passover seder, I put images of Darfur front and center. The purpose of the Passover seder is to tell children the story of the Jewish exodus to freedom. Each year, my family hosts a huge group to listen to us read the story and participate in the accompanying rituals. In 2008, I dedicated the Haggadah, the book from which we read the story, to the children of Darfur. I felt that as Jews around the world celebrated the historical liberation of the Jewish people from the Egyptians who had enslaved them, we needed to remember that even today, not all people are free. Nobody could tell me that the displaced people in Darfur wanted to be in the camps and that the conditions were good. I had seen differently.

As of this writing, the situation in Darfur remains dire. The republic of Sudan is home to more internally displaced people than any other country in the world. Although peace negotiations have resulted in South Sudan's declaration of independence and secession from the rest of the country, conflict continues, and new conflicts have emerged in neighboring Sudanese administrative districts. A full 16.4 percent of all children in the republic of Sudan are acutely malnourished, well above what the world considers "emergency" conditions, and almost 2 million children are suffering from moderate or severe malnutrition.

Political instability, the inability of Western aid organizations to reach impoverished and suffering people, and a decline in funding are all hampering relief efforts. Some areas of Darfur and other regions of the country are now inaccessible to our staff on account of violence.[2] Making the situation worse are diminishing harvests in the country caused by drought and the displacement of farmers. UNICEF has been responding, treating over 75,000 children for acute malnutrition and providing primary health care to at least 6 million people, most of them children. The organization provides emergency water, sanitation, and hygiene services to 1 million people residing in internally displaced camps in Darfur every year. In South Sudan, UNICEF has improved education for 300,000 children, giving nonfood items like blankets and sleeping mats to 1.4 million internally displaced people, and offering psychological support to 70,000 children affected by armed conflict. Yet the needs remain great.

I continue to work on behalf of the people of Darfur and to bear witness wherever political conflict is affecting innocent people. I think often of those powerful women in the desert when I reach out to a woman friend of my own for support. I also recall the strength of these women when I hear my staff say they can't do something. I remind my staff that if women who have so little can build a women's center and influence a large NGO to help fund it, anything is possible.

Darfur has become another image I carry with me wherever I go—an image of hope. Even people in the most hopeless and helpless places manifest a tremendous impulse to work together for the betterment of all. And that means places like Darfur can be turned around someday, because the most important element is already there: the enduring spirit of its people.

3. I BELIEVE IN ZERO

Sierra Leone, Fall 2008

> *For this reason was man created alone, to teach thee*
> *that whosoever destroys a single soul . . . scripture*
> *imputes [guilt] to him as though he had destroyed a*
> *complete world; and whosoever preserves a single*
> *soul . . . scripture ascribes [merit] to him as though he*
> *had preserved a complete world.*

> —TALMUD, SANHEDRIN 37A

ON YOM KIPPUR, the Day of Atonement, Jews around the world attend synagogue services, confess their sins from the previous year, and abstain from food or drink for twenty-four hours to cleanse themselves spiritually. Approaching friends and family members, they admit to transgressions and ask forgiveness. On this holiest of days, they also ask G-d to inscribe them in the Book of Life for the coming year.

When I was a child, I would attend synagogue with members of my family, my friends from Hebrew school, and their families. Some years, my grandfather Leo also joined us. He was a unique man, not too tall, overweight, mostly bald. Born in Poland, he spoke English with a heavy accent, slipping into Yiddish when talking with family members. His smile and eyes were quick; he was perhaps one of the wisest men I have ever known. He was also a devout Jew. Until his death in 1978, he rose early each morning, wound tefillin up his arm and on his head,[1] wrapped his prayer shawl around him, and offered prayers to the G-d he so dearly loved.

On Yom Kippur, I watched Grandpa Leo close his eyes and pray with great intensity, not stopping until the sun went down and the ram's horn—the shofar—sounded to signal the holy day's end. So prayerful was he that his body rocked side to side, as if his supplications to the Divine were delivering him to some distant realm. I felt awed by his steadfast faith, so much so that part of me searched for quite some time to find something to fill my heart and soul the way prayer did his.

As a child, I wasn't as enamored of Yom Kippur as he was. I counted each minute of the holy day, longing for the sun to go down so that my fast could end. Especially tedious was the memorial service, called *Yizkor,* which took place in the afternoon. During Yizkor, the congregation honored and remembered loved ones who had perished, as well as Jews lost during the Holocaust who had left no one behind to remember them. For whatever reason, the temple I attended as a child excused all children from this service. We huddled together outside, waiting for our parents, knowing they would exit teary-eyed, hugging us to help ease the pain of remembering the deceased.

I feel much differently as an adult about Yizkor and the whole Yom Kippur holy day. As I chant the Yizkor service, I recall my dad, whom I so suddenly lost one summer day in 1999, just two months before the birth of my youngest son,

James. I summon up my dad's booming laugh (something I heard often) and can almost feel his six-foot, two-inch frame standing over me and his huge arms wrapped around me. I find myself having imaginary conversations with him, introducing him to all that has gone on this past year, as if I were actually catching up with him. At these moments, I also connect with my grandfather, imagining that I am finally experiencing something like his intensity of prayer as well as a sense of reverence for something bigger than myself or my world. In my busy life, when so much passes by so quickly, the Yizkor service has served me well as a chance to slow down and relish cherished memories—and even more, to process the ongoing transition between the old and the new, the past and the present.

On Yom Kippur 2008, I didn't just chant Yizkor for my dad, other relatives, or other Jews. Having recently returned from a trip to Sierra Leone, one of the poorest countries on Earth, I also prayed for a six-day-old baby girl I had met whose young mother had planned to name Fatima.[2] I screwed my eyes shut, bowed down, and asked G-d for forgiveness. Fatima had died before my very eyes, in a darkened room and in intense pain, with her mother sitting nearby. It was one of the most horrible, heartbreaking things I had ever witnessed, and a death for which I could find no reasonable excuse. As an affluent, intelligent American, I had possessed the means to save this girl, but I hadn't acted in time; no one had. Contravening the Talmudic teaching quoted at the beginning of this chapter, I had stood idly by while an entire world perished.

I had come to Sierra Leone accompanied by executives from Procter & Gamble and the actress Salma Hayek on a goodwill trip conceived in coordination with the Pampers diaper brand. Salma was serving as Procter & Gamble's spokesperson for the Pampers partnership with UNICEF to eliminate maternal and neonatal (MNT) tetanus in developing countries. Our trip to Sierra Leone, accompanied by a crew from ABC's news program *Nightline,* was intended to raise awareness for the campaign and give Salma and myself a chance to see MNT elimination efforts firsthand, so that we could talk about them in an informed way back home. We also wanted to get video footage of Salma in the field that could be used to help promote the campaign.

While I had read the 2008 statistics about neonatal tetanus, and discussed the disease with representatives of Becton, Dickinson and Company (a medical technology company and a leader in the fight against MNT), it was still hard for me to comprehend just what the disease was doing or how we were fighting it: some 140,000 infants and 30,000 mothers were dying each year in places like Sierra Leone—one death every three minutes—from this eminently preventable disease (in developed countries, the disease is rare).[3] Caused by the bacterium *Clostridium tetani,* the disease is transmitted through open wounds arising from unsanitary birthing conditions, usually during the cutting of the umbilical cord. Mothers in developing countries overwhelmingly give birth at home, and unaware of the risk of tetanus, they use anything sharp they have at hand—a piece of metal, a dirty knife—to cut the cord. The mothers often lack access to sanitary environments and the materials required to sterilize tools used during the birthing process.

In theory, the solution is simple. If you inoculate a mother-to-be with two doses of vaccine (by 2012, this was changed to three), she will automatically pass that immunity on to her unborn child, protecting it from the disease, regardless of whether the child is exposed to contaminated utensils or not. The tetanus vaccine itself doesn't even cost that much—around 7 cents per shot, not counting the costs of getting it from the manufacturer and actually administered. The cost on the UNICEF side to procure, deliver, and administer the shot is around 60 cents per shot, $1.20 per woman vaccinated ($1.80 by 2012). Since 2000, UNICEF and its partners have been working to eliminate maternal and neonatal tetanus by providing a series of three doses of the tetanus toxoid vaccine, transportation, health education, and more. By 2008 progress had been swift: 70 million women of childbearing age had been immunized, and eleven new countries (out of the fifty-nine in which tetanus had been rampant in 2000) had eliminated the disease.

But more work remained to be done. In countries like Sierra Leone, mothers still went unvaccinated; babies continued to contract the disease and the result was almost always fatal. In 2006, Procter & Gamble, the manufacturer of Pampers, provided UNICEF with funding for one vaccine for every pack of diapers purchased by a consumer in the United Kingdom. By 2008, the campaign—known as the Pampers-UNICEF "One Pack = One Vaccine" campaign—had spread to U.S. and Canadian markets; the goal was to fund 200 million doses of the vaccine over the next three years (goal increased to 300 million by 2012).

I had decided to visit Sierra Leone because it really was ground zero for infant mortality. Bordering the Atlantic Ocean, Liberia, and Guinea, Sierra Leone is rich in natural resources and known for the harmony that exists between its sizable Muslim and Christian communities. Yet a decade of civil war ending in 2002 had killed tens of thousands of people, left the country's infrastructure in shambles, forced one-third of the population from their homes, and consigned 70 percent of Sierra Leone's population to a life of extreme poverty (under $1 a day in income). Overall life expectancy at the time of our visit was estimated at forty-two years. Democracy was taking hold; presidential and parliamentary elections had taken place in 2007. In their campaign manifestos, all three main political parties recognized the need to improve the plight of the country's children, focusing on education but also on children's rights to protection from violence, exploitation, and abuse.

In 2008 the situation of children in Sierra Leone remained precarious. Recent reports, including the United Nation's Human Development Report, put the country in the bottom strata of development, occupying the unenviable position of last place in human development rankings among 178 countries. Rates of infant and under-five mortality stood among the highest in the world; over 15 percent of infants succumbed at birth and 25 percent of children died before their fifth birthday.[4] Death and disease among children and women of childbearing age stemmed from many factors, including malnutrition, malaria, and acute respiratory infections, but preventable diseases such as tetanus loomed as a primary cause. Only 43 percent of live births took place with the assistance of trained medical staff. Almost half of children received no immunizations, and almost a third of children were moderately or severely underweight and thus susceptible to disease. About a third of all children under five contracted malaria.

UNICEF had been working in Sierra Leone for almost thirty years. For fifteen of those years (1990–2005), the organization's work had focused on providing relief and humanitarian assistance because of the armed conflict engulfing the entire country. In January 2008, UNICEF had started a new three-year program that focused on overall child development. Working with the government, UNICEF was helping to save children's lives and improve their chances of becoming productive members of society by providing improved health services, nutrition, education, water, sanitation, disease control, and protections against exploitation and violence. Hoping to cut under-five and maternal mortality rates by a third, UNICEF was working to train health personnel and provide care to young children and women of childbearing age, including vaccines for preventable diseases like tetanus.

A few weeks before Salma and I left on our trip, I had a chance to meet her at her hotel in New York. I had wondered if I'd find her somewhat aloof, as some celebrities are, but from the start she was warm and engaging, and I quickly decided I was happy to be traveling with her. She had brought her baby, Valentina, with her and before we could find our way into a serious conversation about the work we would do, we forgot our roles, and became two moms comparing notes. We talked about the hardships of soothing our babies when they awakened in the middle of the night; of initially finding breast-feeding more difficult than we expected; of not knowing which piece of parenting advice we hear is actually the one to follow.

This conversation taught me something that I've seen confirmed many times since: parenthood really is a great equalizer. It matters not whether you are a celebrity, a nonprofit executive, or a single mom living in a hut in the bush, the opportunity to talk with another mother is reassuring. We all feel equally inept when we become parents, finding ourselves with more questions than answers, and with a sense that everyone else knows what they're doing but that somehow you weren't given the playbook. We also all change how we see the world after our children are born. Salma told me that this trip took on more meaning now that she was a mother, for she found it unthinkable to lose a child to an easily preventable disease. As she had remarked publicly, "If you knew how to help save a child's life, what could stop you?"

I agreed wholeheartedly; in fact, I was working hard at the time to turn that sentiment into a national obsession. To galvanize public support around the plight of children around the world, I had helped introduce a new campaign our marketing team had created called "I Believe in Zero"—zero deaths of children from preventable causes. As a team, we were proclaiming our collective dismay at how many thousands of children died each day from diseases like neonatal tetanus or poverty-related conditions such as malnutrition or lack of access to clean water. The reported daily number was 26,000—a number so large it was hard to fathom.

The campaign not only focused on the public at large; we intended it as a rallying cry to pull our staff together internally as well. We put up posters around our offices promoting "I Believe in Zero," distributed buttons and T-shirts, and held fun promotional events. Everyone was excited about the campaign, including me. "I Believe in Zero" demanded that we as a staff commit ourselves to reducing that number until it was zero, remembering that the unnecessary death of even one child was unacceptable. We had to become warriors on behalf of the world's vulnerable children, get out there and

fight the good fight. We had set audacious goals; in our strategic plan we committed to doubling our fundraising income in order to bring that 26,000 figure down to zero.

During the weeks before leaving for Sierra Leone, I couldn't
stop thinking about how many babies were dying, how cruel
and unfair it was—and how frustrating it was that the world
wasn't opening up and acknowledging this reality. As
cheerleader-in-chief for the campaign, I tried to think of
new ways of presenting "I Believe in Zero" so Americans and
our own employees would really *feel* the message in their
bones. Was there a way I could help people visualize 26,000
people? Was it the number of people who fit into Yankee Stadium? How many jumbo jets would it take to fly 26,000 passengers? Which university had 26,000 students? I didn't quite
have the answer, but I was confident it would come. Meanwhile, in the background, I found myself continuously thanking G-d that I had my own kids and that they were alive and
well.

As I prepared to leave for Sierra Leone, I suffered from little
anxiety regarding threats to my personal comfort or safety
that had accompanied my earlier trips to developing countries. Was I thrilled about exposure to large and scary tropical bugs? No, but this would be a short trip—only a few
days—and I knew I could handle anything that I was likely
to confront. The many vaccines I would need—yellow fever,
hepatitis A and B, rabies, typhoid, polio—didn't faze me. I
filled my malarone prescription, started my pills, and only
spent a rare few moments worrying. Travel to the field was
starting to seem like old hat, and that in itself felt good. My
family wasn't nearly as concerned about this trip as they had

been about my travel to Darfur. "Oh, okay, she's leaving again," seemed to be the general attitude.

Still, the notion that we were doing something at least a little dangerous emerged the day before our scheduled departure. I was attending a reception hosted by the Congressional Black Caucus for board members of the Martin Luther King Jr. Memorial in Washington, D.C. I love serving on this board, not only because the mission is dear to my heart or because I have been privileged to be the first white woman asked to join it, but also because the people on the board always go out of their way to make me feel welcome. At the reception, attended by then Senator Barack Obama, I told board members that I was about to leave for Sierra Leone. "Really?" they said. "It's dangerous over there. You're out of your mind!" At one point, I had a chance to chat with Obama about my kids and my former work at the Anti-Defamation League. When I told him I was going to Sierra Leone, he, too, told me to be careful and wished me "Godspeed." Perhaps just a little part of me was thinking yet again: "What have I gotten myself into?"

Our group—including Salma, myself, the Procter & Gamble executives, *Nightline* coanchor Cynthia McFadden, *Nightline* senior broadcast producer and cameraman Almin Karamehmedovic (who planned to do a segment on the trip), and Salma's manager—landed in Freetown, Sierra Leone's capital, and were met on the tarmac by our UNICEF country team. Joining them were members of my New York team, Deanna Helmig from our corporate relations department and Lisa Szarkowski, who had flown in earlier to scout out potential locations for filming. Lisa told us that she had arranged for us to visit with a baby suffering from tetanus; she had acquired the infection from a dirty knife used to cut her umbilical cord. The visit would ensure that ABC's *Nightline* and Salma truly understood the human impact of the disease.

Our photographer had been exploring Freetown and discovered the baby; it is rare to find a baby suffering from tetanus, since they usually die so quickly. After lengthy deliberation with the UNICEF Sierra Leone team, the hospital staff, and, most important, the baby's mother, a decision was made to allow a very small group to visit the baby. We appreciated the many sensitivities involved in taking a group of foreigners to see a sick baby, but the medical staff believed the baby would survive, and we all thought the good that could be done by making Americans more aware of tetanus would outweigh any negative consequences. We anticipated being able to see hospital staff administer treatment to the child—this way, American viewers would get a sense of how easy it was to control the disease and prevent horrific human suffering. We agreed to skip our hotel (and the hot showers we so desperately needed) and go straight to Freetown's only children's hospital.

We received a reminder—if any was needed—that we were not in the United States or another developed country. Our two pilots, who hadn't been to a developing nation before, were planning to park the plane at the airport, go sightseeing while we were gone, and visit a market to reprovision our plane for the return trip. Someone from the airport came over and tapped them on the shoulder: "Uh-uh, you can't leave this plane here. Someone has to stay with it at all times."

"Why?" one of our pilots asked.

"If you don't stay here, the plane won't be here when you get back. It will be stripped bare of all parts."

Much to their disappointment, our pilots kept watch over the aircraft. Meanwhile, the rest of us flew by helicopter to a parking area, where we boarded jeeps for the drive to the hospital.

Sierra Leone's beauty is readily apparent from the air. Mountains rise in the distance beyond Freetown, the city's peninsula forming Africa's largest natural harbor. Blue-green water meets sand beach that in turn gives way to a lush, tropical greenery. In Freetown, however, the poverty left in the wake of the brutal civil war that raged between 1991 and 2002 quickly becomes apparent. Out the window of our jeep, I saw people and animals thronging the streets, as well as garbage and raw sewage. On the main roads, motorbikes and buses jammed with people passed by between rows of low, open-air stalls stacked one against the other. In these stalls, merchants sold products like bananas or roasted corn; the stalls also functioned as makeshift hair salons or other kinds of service businesses.

The children's hospital was a fairly substantial, modern building—much larger than we expected, with tile floors, glass windows, and electricity for ceiling fans. Yet it had no bathrooms, was not air-conditioned, and was lit only by bare light bulbs. A stench of body odor suffused the place.

Members of the hospital staff led us through a ward, a scene I can only describe as heart-wrenching. We were warned that we would encounter children with severe burns. Many of Sierra Leone's homes lack electricity, so families use oil lamps for light. Unfortunately these tip over, and the oil and resulting fires cause severe burns. The children here were sleeping on floor mats covered by pale blue bed nets, writhing in pain and moaning indescribably. Lacking even the most basic pain medications, doctors and nurses could only treat infections as they arose and hope the children eventually healed.

The mothers of the children attended to their day-to-day needs. Few nurses worked at the hospital, leaving the mothers to bathe their children, pick up their waste, and prepare their meals on fires they lit outside the building. You could see how emotionally and physically spent these women were, witnessing their children's anguish, yet lacking tools to ease their pain. Lacking child care, some mothers had other, healthy children in the ward with them, who also required their attention. Nothing I had seen compared with the intensity of human suffering here. Unfortunately, we were just getting started.

We walked through the ward, trying to smile at the children, making eye contact with each mom. At the far end, we reached a little room with cinder-block walls where the baby suffering from tetanus was. We took turns going in, and as I awaited my turn, I did my best to educate the others about what they would be seeing. The nurse came by and asked if we had any questions. I asked her when the hospital staff would be able to administer drugs to save the baby.

"Oh, we won't be able to do that," she said, matter-of-factly.

"Why not?"

"Our best hope would be to administer an antitoxin to counteract the toxin in this baby's body. But we can't get it. Everywhere we've called, they don't have it. That little child will live or die by the grace of G-d. Almost certainly, she will die."

"You've called everywhere?"

"Everywhere in Sierra Leone."

"How long does the baby have?"

"It could be an hour, or it could be a day."

She walked away, leaving me dumbfounded. I couldn't believe that in this entire country, they couldn't come up with a single dose of the drug that might help save this child. But that was the reality. And to the nurse, this situation was nothing exceptional. It was everyday life.

A pall fell over our group. When it came time for me to enter, I found the little room extremely dark—no windows or lights. The air was stale. According to the medical personnel, the disease had heightened the baby's senses so much that even the slightest bit of light caused distress. Noise or touch felt excruciating, too; the mother was not allowed to even hold her child or sing to her. She was instead left to helplessly watch.

I approached the small crib (a rarity in the hospital) to find a tiny, six-day-old infant, her fists clenched in pain. Every few moments, the child convulsed, her whole body jerking. A tiny feeding tube ran into her nostril, and she wore a cloth diaper. Her mother, sitting nearby in a chair, was despondent. I was struck by how young she looked, and yet how old. She couldn't have been much older than nineteen or twenty, but her face and body were imprinted with suffering; she seemed to be aging before my eyes. A purple scarf covered her hair, and she wore earrings and a green T-shirt. As we had learned, this was her first baby and she was terrified. She had walked alone to a rural health clinic and had been referred here.

I nodded to her, sitting down in a nearby chair. She smiled wanly and uttered words I couldn't understand. She didn't speak English, so we couldn't really have a conversation without the help of an interpreter. Given the dire situation, attempting an elaborate process of translation seemed too much. In any case, this poor mother had little to say. Her baby was desperately ill; anything else was utterly irrelevant.

I took her hand. "I'm really sorry about your baby."

She probably didn't comprehend my words, but she took hold of my hand anyway and continued to hold it.

Minutes passed. The room itself was silent save for the moaning coming from the ward next door and the rasping sound of the infant's difficult breathing. There was nothing for me to do but just sit like this, holding the hand of a woman I'd just met, while together we watched her child suffer.

I took several deep breaths, registering the gravity of the situation, all the while knowing that this moment was repeating itself dozens of times each day around the globe. And also knowing that if it were my child suffering back in New York, the situation would be altogether different. If my child showed symptoms of tetanus, medications to combat the disease and ease its symptoms would be available to him immediately.

It was horrifying, feeling so completely impotent. I looked from the baby to the mother and back to the baby. Time seemed to stand still as I got lost in trying to fully imagine what this young woman was feeling. When your child hurts, as a mom, *you* hurt. This baby was so clearly in agony that even I, a perfect stranger, found it unbearable to watch. I closed my eyes, saying silent prayers, and hoping for some sort of miraculous recovery.

Over the course of a few minutes, I became aware that the raspy sound the baby had been making seemed to have stopped. Moving my head a bit closer to the crib, I saw that the baby had grown very still. I watched as the color drained right out of her hand, and I knew she was dead. Her mother, whose hand I still held in mine, had not yet realized what had happened, even though she was still watching her baby. I didn't know what to do. I had never witnessed the moment of death before. Should I leave? Should I tell the mother what had happened? Should I get someone?

A nurse came in and took the baby's hand, shaking it in an attempt to wake her. I walked out of the room because I realized the nurse would have to tell the mother. As I exited, I heard the mother wailing. I will never forget the pure agony in her voice.

Lisa went in after me and confirmed that the baby had died. We all felt the loss of this child we hadn't known. An overwhelming sense of helplessness and despair came over me. If we had been in the United States, this baby—and twenty-six thousand others like her who die daily of easily preventable causes like neonatal tetanus—might not have died. A doctor or otherwise trained medical professional would have cut her umbilical cord with a sterile instrument, and basic medication would have sufficed to help the baby get well even if she had fallen ill with tetanus. This baby was six days old. *Six days*. Her mother had tried everything possible to get the best care for her. This was just the way things were—and it was impossible to accept. I understood now the full horror and helplessness associated with child mortality, gaining more resolve than ever to bring the number of children dying each day all the way down to zero.

To help calm us down, a doctor took us into a nearby room and offered us a bit more information about what had happened. He was a small man, dark-skinned, and wearing a doctor's white coat. "It is so frustrating, I cannot tell you," he said, wrenching his hands. "This illness is both treatable and preventable. The only thing we could give her was some Valium to control her spasms. We were desperate to save this baby, but there was nothing else."

"And this happens all the time?"

"All the time. We just don't have the tools we need in this country. And as a result, babies are dying. It's not right, but it is happening. We need to do better. These children are our future; without them, we have nothing."

It was time to go. We rode in silence to our next stop, a reception with Sierra Leone's first lady. We were all very upset, reflecting on and digesting what we had seen. Later that evening, we began dinner by talking a bit about the day's events and holding a moment of silence for little Fatima.

The next morning, we crammed ourselves into a rickety helicopter for a half-hour trip to Makeni, a small town in central Sierra Leone where UNICEF helps support the Binkolo Maternal Health Center, a place for women to receive routine care, including birthing facilities, vaccinations, and prenatal care. And just like that, we were jerked from the horrific to the sublime.

Greeting us as we emerged from the helicopter was a group of six little girls ranging from six to twelve years of age, all wearing crisp white dresses and carrying bouquets of pink flowers. These were healthy kids who had come to greet Salma. They didn't know who she was, although they did seem to know that she was a famous actress. They surrounded her on a muddy field and sang a welcome song to us in little high-pitched voices to an African rhythm. We couldn't understand the words very well (the words "peace and unity" stood out), but the emotion was so sweet that I couldn't help but smile.

After the greeting, we went to another clinic and a school before driving to a remote village, which was far from a health facility; we wanted to understand the realities facing many women in Sierra Leone lacking regular access to health care. Suddenly the impoverished places we had seen earlier that day looked far more impressive, reminding me that poverty has levels—that even those who have so little can feel rich in comparison to those who have less. Here, members of the community came with their children to a central location to receive basic services, including tetanus immunizations. Walking to an open-air building in the middle of a circle of traditional mud huts, we found long lines of mothers waiting quietly to get immunized. They held babies in their arms or carried them on their backs, and other children grabbed at their legs. Health-care workers were weighing and measuring babies to check for malnutrition, while others triaged sick children, making sure they received whatever care was available.

The UNICEF team and local health workers patiently explained the vaccination process to Salma. "It is not that hard," a health worker said, handing Salma a pair of latex gloves to put on. "First, you put the serum into the syringe, like this." He took the syringe and jabbed the needle into the tetanus serum, drawing the plunger up slowly so as to fill the syringe with vaccine. "You withdraw the exact amount—see, up to this line."

Salma looked at where his finger was pointing, and he continued. "Next, move the needle up into the air and tap the side of the syringe to loosen any air bubbles. You should press the plunger until liquid drips or squirts from the needle's tip." He demonstrated this for her. "Of course, you need to clean the injection site, using one of these." He held up an alcohol wipe. "And then, you hold the syringe at a ninety-degree angle over the injection site, insert the needle, and look to see if any blood comes out. If so, pull back the plunger and see if any blood comes into the syringe. If it does, then you've hit a vein."

"Is that a problem?" I asked.

He nodded yes. "You don't want to give a vaccine right into a vein. It won't hurt the person, but it will render the vaccine useless."

This was news to me; I had never really thought about where injections were actually given.

"Tetanus bacteria live in the muscles," he went on to explain, "not in the blood being carried through our veins. The bacteria will not grow if there is oxygen present, and there is oxygen in the blood. So if you hit a vein, you need to withdraw and start again."

Interesting. I'd watched immunizations many times and had never known this.

He concluded his demonstration. "When you're sure you're in a muscle, you push the plunger all the way in with your thumb and it's done!"

He demonstrated on the next two women before he presented a young woman for Salma to inoculate. We all stood behind her, watching. She seemed completely at ease as she followed the health-care worker's instructions and injected the young mother-to-be, who then moved off the long line. The *Nightline* crew hurriedly captured the entire thing on film. Salma had tears in her eyes as she turned to us, and we all applauded. We may have just witnessed a life being saved.

We spent several more hours at the clinic, talking to the mothers waiting in line. We asked questions about their children: How old were they? How many siblings did they have? Were they walking or talking yet? The women looked so young to us; most were in their late teens or early twenties and already had one or two children. When we told them why we were there, they described their experiences with tetanus. One woman told us how as a midwife she was overcome with frustration watching mothers and babies become infected and die from tetanus. We understood; we had witnessed it ourselves.

We took a walk through a village nearby—thatched-roof huts scattered between thick trees surrounding a central clearing. At random, we selected a woman to speak with whose story—told as she held a baby in her arms—seemed to summarize our day. "I lost my first child to tetanus. A boy. He was only days old. I did not think I would recover from the pain. I got the vaccination because I came to the clinic with my friend who was getting one. G-d blessed me with another baby. This one is healthy. I gave birth to him four weeks ago."

There it was. The difference a vaccination campaign can make. It wasn't just a bunch of numbers. It was an individual woman whose baby would now live.

A long conversation had begun between Lisa and me as soon as we left Freetown that would continue for many days. While each of us struggled for words to express what we had felt watching a baby die, we were finding it much easier to discuss it intellectually, in a way that separated ourselves from the event itself. At first this seemed appropriate, since it allowed us each to continue working, but it left us wondering how we would share this experience upon our return to the United States.

We had had a videographer filming at the hospital for the two days that Fatima struggled. We debated whether or not the footage should be shared with a mass audience. We agreed, as we had before visiting the hospital, that our first priority was respecting the dignity of Fatima and her mother. This was their story, not ours. While we had permission to share it, we had entered into the agreement to film never believing Fatima would die. Was it fair to show such an intimate moment? But if the footage was presented appropriately, most of us thought that the story should be told, even showing Fatima's death. We had come here to learn, to get an understanding of what tetanus was doing to children around the globe. We were not only shocked by what we had seen; we were shocked that we had not been aware of it before this trip. How could a disease, especially one so painful and so easily preventable, still be allowed to infect babies? If our goal was to engage Americans in doing something about it, wouldn't showing the footage produce more results than anything else? But could the American public cope with seeing what we had seen?

As this discussion proceeded, I experienced so many complex emotions. What I most wanted was to stop talking and run home, see my own kids, and hug them. My heart ached for Fatima, but I also felt immense gratitude that I as a mom had never faced what Fatima's mother had—that my kids had been born where they were born, thereby ensuring their safe arrival. I longed to be back in the comfort of their company, secure in the knowledge that they were safe and sound. I also felt selfish and guilty for having these thoughts, aware that Fatima's mother would leave the hospital empty-handed.

I remember the rest of the trip—meeting other women, having conversations, holding babies, playing with children. But this one day, which began with the death of one child and ended with the saving of another, truly overshadowed everything else. When we boarded our plane for the return trip to Europe, tears streamed down all our faces. We were relieved to be going back to an easier life, and at the same time, we were mourning a child we barely knew, but who had changed each of us forever.

The emotions intensified even further when I returned to the United States. The day I got back, September 30, was my father's birthday. I found myself struggling anew with thoughts of loss.

I had been seven and a half months pregnant with our son James when I received the call back in 1999 telling me that my dad had collapsed. He had not been ill; it had happened out of the blue. Oddly, the morning of his death, he had happened to call me, and we had talked for almost an hour. This in itself was unusual. My father wasn't one for phone calls; it was my mom who served as the communicator among us all. But that morning, almost as if he had foreseen what the afternoon would bring, he called. We talked about my work, his golf game, what Lee (then four years old) was doing, Donald's latest real estate investments, and the family outing we had planned for that afternoon. As usual, we teased one another and I laughingly said he should call me more. We ended by saying "I love you," and I hung up with a smile on my face.

I rounded up Donald and Lee and went out with our neighbors Sally and Joe and their four-year-old, Drew. We spent the afternoon together, having pizza at a local restaurant and ice cream at Carvel. At six in the evening, we returned home. The call came as Donald went upstairs to our room and I began to get Lee ready for his bath. Feeling the weight of my unborn baby along with exhaustion from a day on my feet, I moved slowly to grab the phone and was happy to hear my brother say hello. With no warning, the hammer fell. "Caryl, they have just taken Dad away in an ambulance. It doesn't look good. He's hemorrhaging internally. There's blood everywhere."

I have relived that defining moment so many times I've lost count. My world seemed to turn completely upside down, yet strangely, I was aware that life kept on moving normally for others around us. Cars kept honking on our street outside, people continued with their dinners, my husband was still upstairs changing his clothes, completely unaware of what had happened.

I called around for flights. I was so distraught—and so pregnant—that I wasn't sure I could fly. There was only one remaining flight that evening. I was having difficulty breathing and wasn't sure what to do. I called my brother back. "Look, tell me the truth, is he alive? Because there's one flight, with only one seat left, and I have twenty-four minutes to make it, which I will do if he is alive. There isn't enough time to make arrangements for Lee, so I will have to come alone, and I am shaking terribly right now. What should I do?"

He hung up and a moment later, my mom called. "He's

gone, Caryl." She was too distraught to say much more. I later learned that he had been sitting in his chair in their den, watching golf on TV, while my mom was cooking dinner in the kitchen. Mom heard him cough, and when she went to see if he was okay, found him collapsed and hemorrhaging. The room was a mess, covered with my father's blood. She called for help, and miraculously a neighbor heard and came running. My father was alive when the ambulance arrived, but he died on the way to the hospital.

When I heard my dad was gone, I dropped to the floor and wailed. Lee ran into the room. "Mommy, Mommy, are you okay?" I couldn't catch my breath enough to talk to him, and in any case, I didn't have the words to explain what was going on. Lee says he had never seen me cry before that day. I don't think I got off the floor for well over an hour. I just sat there and sobbed, even though it continued to terrify Lee. I kept telling Lee through my tears that it was okay, but it wasn't okay. I wanted to console Lee, but I couldn't find the strength. The pain was so deep that it took every bit of energy just to stay where I was and experience it.

I remember my husband running to me and trying to help. Somewhere in the back of my mind, I knew I had to get up and pull myself together. I had to make flight arrangements, pack a bag, and call others to tell them what happened. I eventually did all of those things, but as my body went through the motions, my mind begged me to go back to the moment when I had first answered the phone and heard my brother's voice—the moment before I knew I had lost my dad.

I thought of all this as I arrived back in New York City, aware that it connected me to what Fatima's mother might have felt as she wailed. It was the same deep sadness that had come out of me the evening my father had died. I wanted to turn around—to go back to Sierra Leone and embrace that poor woman.

Of course, I had no right to do that. I didn't know Fatima's mother, didn't speak her language, didn't know if she would want to see me again or if she even remembered me holding her hand. For her, I imagine, time had stopped in that small room in the hospital. Perhaps she, too, wondered how the rest of the world had kept moving. Had she been any more prepared for what took place that day than I had been when my father died? When she brought her baby to the hospital, had it even entered her head that she might not bring her back home? Likewise, how could I now return to my life as usual, now that I knew that this one baby in Sierra Leone was no longer with us? It just didn't make any sense.

Not even a week after returning home, I was packed and out the door again, this time bound for Dubai as a guest of the University of Pennsylvania's Wharton Fellowship Program. I was traveling with a group of bright, ambitious, mostly young alumni who had taken what I call "downtown jobs"— positions with salaries that dwarfed mine, even though I had more than double their work experience. Dressed mostly in designer clothes, and far more accustomed than I to enjoying the finest food, drink, and vacations that life had to offer, they had come to Dubai to learn about the country's burgeoning economy and its many development and investment opportunities.

I found it disconcerting to be in Dubai. Once a small town of Bedouin traders, this city in the middle of the desert today mixes old-world charm with modern architecture and extreme wealth. Dubai reminds me of a more elite version of Las Vegas. Both are adult fantasy lands, with ample opportunities to live large. Whereas Las Vegas has its casinos, in Dubai I found seven-star properties, the world's tallest tower, manmade islands in various shapes aimed at enticing a buyer's imagination, even underwater hotels and an indoor ski slope. It was opulent beyond my wildest imagination.

Our hosts wined and dined us, including a cocktail party in a suite at the top of the Burj Hotel. Soaring to a height of 321 meters and designed to conjure up the image of a sailboat, the Burj has repeatedly been voted the world's most luxurious hotel. I could barely contain my amazement in the lobby as we encountered deep blue floor tiles and walls, set off by the bright yellows and reds in the carpets and lavish furnishings—a mix of modern and Middle Eastern styles. The uninterrupted view from the suite of the sea and the city was simply spectacular. Later, we were herded into private golf carts and given tours of sites at which amusement parks and golf courses were being constructed. Our hosts also carted us onto yachts to get a closer look at the private islands up for sale.

Our hosts had set out to impress us, and it was working. Most of the group was intoxicated by what they were seeing. On many levels, so was I; it was just so amazing. But I could not let go of where I had just been, as if the two trips had been set up as deliberate foils of one another. Perhaps if I had reversed the trips—had come to Dubai first and then Sierra Leone—I would have relished this opportunity more and enjoyed living in the lap of luxury. But I had just watched a baby die. I found myself calculating in my head how many lives could have been saved with the money used to create this opulence. I knew such thinking was unreasonable and unfair, but I could not help myself.

It wasn't only in Dubai. Back in New York, the image of a little hand with the color draining out of it stayed with me. I was unsettled and struggling to keep my composure. In the middle of a speech I gave at a benefit ball for UNICEF, I burst into tears before hundreds of people. On another occasion, I called an all-staff meeting and told them Fatima's story, concluding by saying, "So in the weeks to come when you think that we're asking too much or that the demands on us are too high, just remember why we're doing it." I cried that day in front of my staff for the first time. Other people on our team cried, too. We all got the message. Our purpose was to help save kids whom we had the power to save but who lacked a voice in the world. We had to ask ourselves: how can we let these kids die? And we had to proclaim, loud enough for an entire country to hear: something is happening here, and no, it is not okay. We believe in zero.

The words "I Believe in Zero" were no longer just a catchy campaign slogan for me. They were real. Although I had felt committed to my work before, I now knew what it felt like to have to look another mother in the eye, knowing her child had just perished needlessly. I found the image I had been seeking to communicate the essence of the campaign, an image powerful enough to break through to our fellow Americans and convince them to act. I understood that I could use my voice to make a difference, and I was determined to do so.

If I could save even one child like Fatima, bring that 26,000 down just a little bit, I would have been pleased—but not at all satisfied. I now fully grasped the fact that for every one of those children that make up that 26,000, there was a mother, a father, a sister, aunt, or grandmother whose world would stop the way mine did the day my dad died, who would feel a hole in their lives now that this child was no longer with them. While we couldn't do anything about those who had already died, there was a lot we could do to save the ones still living. And we needed to do it quicker and better than we ever thought possible.

As of this writing, some four years after my Sierra Leone visit, we're making important progress against tetanus. More than $40 million has been contributed, enabling UNICEF to procure over 300 million vaccines to protect more than 100 million women and their future newborns. Working with partners and funders, UNICEF has helped eliminate MNT in fifteen more countries since 2008: Burundi, Comoros, Republic of the Congo, Turkey, Benin, Mozambique, Myanmar, Ghana, Liberia, Senegal, Uganda, Burkina Faso, Guinea-Bissau, Tanzania, and Timor-Leste. This is the kind of progress we yearn for, and which would not be possible without the many partners who contribute to UNICEF's global MNT elimination program. In 2010, Kiwanis International—backed by its membership of nearly 600,000 volunteers—joined global efforts by partnering with UNICEF and launching The Eliminate Project. They are an exciting addition to the MNT Elimination initiative, which is an international private-public partnership that includes national governments, UNICEF, WHO, UNFPA, GAVI, USAID/Immunization Basics, CDC, UNICEF National Committees, the government of Japan, Save the Children, PATH, RMHC, the Bill & Melinda Gates Foundation, Kiwanis International, Pampers (a division of Procter & Gamble), and BD.

Meanwhile, the number of children dying every day from all preventable causes has declined to about 19,000, down from 33,000 in 1991. That's quite a positive development for the human race, but it's still not good enough. Even today, millions of children are not reaching their fifth birthday. Worse, they are dying of preventable causes and treatable diseases. And the majority of those deaths are concentrated among the poorest 20 percent of households in the developing world. In fact, half of all global child deaths occur in just five countries: India, Nigeria, Democratic Republic of Congo, Pakistan, and China. UNICEF is redoubling efforts to serve those most in need, based on our knowledge that each $1 million invested in a country with high mortality rates can potentially prevent 60 percent more deaths. With enough resources and commitment, UNICEF can reach all these children. At the U.S. Fund for UNICEF we won't stop at "fewer" deaths. We believe in zero.

4. WHAT WE TEACH OUR CHILDREN

Brazil, August 2009

Our similarities bring us to a common ground; our differences allow us to be fascinated by each other.

—TOM ROBBINS

CHILDREN IN DEVELOPING COUNTRIES aren't just victims. Sometimes they are heroes who prove themselves every bit as capable of changing our lives as we are of changing theirs.

I learned this lesson while sitting in the conference room of a hotel in the Brazilian city of Manaus, in the Amazon Basin. Surrounding me were seven American women and their children, as well as my oldest son, Lee. The American children, ages ten to fifteen, were getting fidgety. They had arrived only the day before, and this was their first time in a developing country. Struggling to adapt to an unfamiliar place, they were more interested in their electronic gadgets than they were in our mission—learning firsthand about the plight of children around the world.

The door opened, and a Brazilian boy entered. He was fifteen years old, but with his slight build, bushy brown hair, whimsical eyes, and endearing smile, he looked younger than that, perhaps twelve. He was dressed modestly in neat blue jeans and a white short-sleeved polo shirt. Our children noticed his entry, but didn't do much to acknowledge it. The tapping on their iPods continued.

A member of the Brazil UNICEF team asked for quiet, handed this boy a microphone, and prompted him to introduce himself. "Hello," he said in English, looking primarily at the ground. He spoke the word quietly, haltingly, and with a strong accent; I could tell he wasn't used to addressing groups, certainly not English-speaking Americans.

"Tell them your name and a little about why you're here," our host said in Portuguese.

The boy cleared his throat. Still looking at the ground, and amidst continued background whispering from our children, he spoke through an interpreter. "My name is RC [name changed]. I live in Manaus. I traveled a long way to get here today. I'm proud to be here."

At this, some of our children looked over and began to pay attention.

"I came because I thought it was important for the Americans to hear my story. I don't remember a time in my life when I wasn't sick. Even as a child, I was sick a lot."

Now everyone was looking up; this was more interesting than the same old video game.

"I never knew what my sickness was, but I knew that whatever it was, I wasn't supposed to talk about it. My mother said not to. When I got older, I learned that I was HIV-positive."

The room fell silent. No whispers. No clicking of buttons or shifting of bodies in chairs. RC continued to tell his story, and all of us, adults and children, became utterly absorbed.

None of us would ever be the same, so powerful were his words and our intimate contact with his honest emotions. My assumptions about what kids in industrialized countries can learn and feel, and about what I as a parent had an obligation to teach, would be transformed forever.

We had come to Brazil as a result of some personal reflections I had around the time I visited Sierra Leone. I found myself taking stock of just how much my life had changed these past few years. Working at the U.S. Fund had forced me to push far beyond my comfort zone, but it was more than that. I had crossed some imaginary line I had created, finding a part of myself I didn't know existed, discovering a strength I didn't know I had.

It wasn't easy fitting this new self-awareness into my everyday life as a mom in America. I cringed each evening when I cleaned up after supper and threw away perfectly good leftovers because "broccoli is not something I like, Mom." I also felt a more urgent desire to ensure that my own children understood just how privileged their lives were. My friend and U.S. Fund board member Sherrie Westin calls it "inculcating a discipline of gratitude" in our children: teaching them to be thankful. I wondered how we as parents did that, whether it should be part of what our schools teach— whether it was even possible for us to teach it at all.

I knew I was not alone in pondering these issues. We all want our children to have everything we can give them, but we also want them to appreciate what they have. Most people I knew who had returned to the United States after working in the field struggled to find the right balance. One woman told me that when she was in Africa, she borrowed the office

VCR every Friday night, and her kids squealed in delight to see one of the three English children's television tapes some-one had sent her. Within months of returning to New York, however, she heard them complaining that there was noth-ing to watch on the hundred-plus cable channels available to them. It made me wonder: are there times when less is just so much more?

Shortly after returning from Sierra Leone, in the fall of 2008, I had lunch with Sherrie at a restaurant on the Upper West Side of Manhattan, near her office. We had traveled to Mozambique together, and her daughter Lily was the same age as my son Lee. As we ate our salads, Sherrie and I rem-inisced about what an incredible, eye-opening experience Mozambique had been, and we confessed how much we wished we could explain it to our children. Sherrie's eyes widened as an idea came to her. "Why don't we do a family trip of us moms with our kids?"

Now my eyes were widening. "Could we really do that? If I brought Lee, would you really bring Lily?"

At first, it didn't look like the trip would happen. When I raised the idea at a senior management team meeting held in my office, my four other team members looked at me as if I'd lost my mind. The liability issues alone were daunting. What if a child got sick or hurt on the trip? Wouldn't we be re-sponsible? Heaven forbid a child died.

Another of my colleagues shook his head. "You're talking about exposing these kids to difficult living conditions and diseases. Would they even want to go? Would their parents want to spend the money?"

"Is it even worth the trouble?" a third asked. "What pur-pose is being served here?"

I told my colleagues that I thought the trip was worth

taking. "We want our donors to see UNICEF projects first-hand. If their kids are involved and inspired, think how much more committed they will be to what we do. And if we engage kids at this age, think about how committed *they* will be as they get older."

I'm not sure I convinced anyone that day, but we did agree to compile a list of donors who just might be enticed to take such a trip. I would arrange meetings and at least float the idea by everyone on the list. I wasn't certain what response I would receive. As it turned out, our donors loved the idea of taking their kids into the field. Every woman I approached wanted to go. Nobody said, "I don't think it's appropriate to take my kids to a developing country" or "That's not what I want to do with my children." All told, eight women ex-pressed interest, including Sherrie, myself, an executive at one of our large corporate partners, a prominent television news anchor, a film actress (also a member of our board), and three other strong supporters of UNICEF.

As members of my team found ways to overcome the lia-bility and logistical issues, we started thinking about where to take the trip. I was adamant that the children get a real field experience, but that we also attend to their basic crea-ture comforts. I didn't want the kids to feel so scared or un-comfortable that the point of the experience got lost. We also needed to choose a country that would allow our kids to witness substantial issues affecting children, but where they wouldn't experience health risks themselves. Ideally, the travel would not be too long or require a change of planes, nor did I want our kids to have to adjust to a major time zone shift. We wound up choosing Brazil, and specifically, the Amazon Basin area near the city of Manaus.

Brazil is an incredibly complex country, one of the

fastest-growing economies in the world, as well as a progressive society in many respects. Physically, the country is enormous; all of Europe would fit inside its boundaries. However, the country still had pockets of extreme poverty. The most recent UNICEF country report on Brazil revealed that approximately 60 million Brazilians (out of 190 million) lived in poverty, including roughly 13 million children in the semiarid and 9 million children in the Amazon region. Even with Brazil's status as a middle-income country, about 44,000 children in the country died each year before their fifth birthday, mostly from preventable diseases and complications related to malnutrition. The report further explained that about 40 percent of the mothers in Brazil still did not receive adequate prenatal care; this contributed to the high child mortality rates.

I found it disturbing to learn that regional and racial inequity remained a major problem in Brazil. Children of African heritage apparently experienced a 40 percent greater chance of dying as infants than their white counterparts, with children of indigenous tribes having a 138 percent higher chance of dying. The report joined others in praising Brazil's response to the HIV/AIDS crisis as one of world's best. Still, approximately 330,000 adolescents in the country were living with HIV, and even more troubling, half of all new HIV infections affected adolescents and youth between the ages of fifteen and twenty-four years old. As I looked across the table at my own teenage child, that statistic hit home.

HIV/AIDS was hardly the only issue plaguing Brazil's children. Child care and education were also big challenges. According to the country report, only 7.5 percent of children under three in the region we would visit, the Amazon states, attended any sort of formal day-care center, even though there were few adults to watch over them during the work-day. This left a huge number of children without any adult supervision whatsoever while their parents went out to earn money. I tried to imagine leaving Lee in charge of his younger brother, James, while I went to the office. I had spent endless hours selecting the right child care for them, and both had attended preschools.

Children in Brazil who found their way to a school often did not get the privilege of completing their education. In some regions, only a small percentage managed to stay in school during their high school years. Some lacked the sup-port to stay; others were pulled out to watch their younger siblings or to work to help support their families.

But it was Brazil's child protection issues that I found hard-est to read about. In the United States, state and federal gov-ernments use census data and birth registration data to help allocate resources. In Brazil, hundreds of thousands of chil-dren were never issued birth certificates, leaving them with-out access to any sort of public services. They were literally people without citizenship, vulnerable to criminals who would prey upon them: when you do not legally exist, no one takes legal notice if you go missing. You might die a violent death at a young age, and no one would care enough to even look into the incident. One report I read stated that more than 8,000 kids and adolescents had died in homicides in 2005, with the majority of their cases not reported or inves-tigated.

UNICEF had been on the ground in Brazil for over sixty years, and this trip would give our donors an opportunity to see the organization's work firsthand. I wasn't sure if our kids would fully understand it. It would be easy to explain what UNICEF's health work was all about, but I didn't know if our kids would appreciate the advocacy efforts that helped to ensure the rights of children and improve their lives. I also worried about how I would explain the HIV/AIDS issues to our kids. How much did they already know about the disease—and how much *should* they know? I couldn't predict how they would react to meeting children their age who were infected with the virus or living with the disease.

Still, when we had worked out all the details with UNICEF's Brazil office, I was so excited that I went straight home to tell Lee. He was fourteen and attended the UN International School (UNIS), so being in a foreign place did not feel especially daunting to him. He did have a number of concerns. Would we stay in a hotel? Would he need a backpack? How would he dress? Could he wear jeans? Could he bring his iPod? What would he actually *do* there? Would he get a chance to meet Brazilian kids? How many shots would he have to get at the doctor's office before leaving? I answered all these questions, realizing that this was good practice; the other mothers and kids would likely have similar conversations. But an alarm bell went off inside me: I wasn't sure these kids would really be able to handle the physical act of traveling to a developing country. If they resisted it, we would all have an awful time. Pushing this anxiety aside, I took notes on all he asked so that I could be sure to share the answers with the other women.

Other anxieties came out when I took Lee to a travel doctor to get his immunizations several weeks before we left. As we sat in the waiting room, I read a brochure about immunizations and my mind started racing. *What if all these shots make him sick? Will he run a fever?* It got worse when we saw the doctor and I asked if Lee needed a rabies vaccine. The doctor shrugged her shoulders. "Well, it's not like you'll be coming in contact with rabid animals, right?"

"We'll be on a boat going up the Rio Negro and in rural villages. Who knows what we'll come across?"

The doctor looked up at me. "You're going *where*? The Amazon River Basin? Darn right he ought to consider a rabies vaccination. Only problem is, it's almost impossible to get one in the United States. I am going to give him hepatitis A and B, a polio booster, rubella, typhoid, and yellow fever vaccines."

Lee didn't seem especially upset at hearing that he might contract rabies. I think he was just glad to be getting one less shot. But the doctor's reaction shook me up. *Damn,* I said to myself, *do I really know what I'm doing here?*

Ultimately, I did think I was making a good parenting choice. Beyond bridging the emotional disconnect between my work experiences and home life, taking a family trip such as this would allow me to address in some small way the parental guilt that had long nagged at me about having to travel so much. I had always enjoyed the traveling, but I was also pained that it took me away from my growing children. I wouldn't have been able to take the CEO job at all had it not been for the generosity and dedication of my husband. When I was in the running for the position, Donald and I talked about what the heavy travel would mean for our family. Donald assured me that he would fill in for me when I was gone, but in return he expected me to try really hard to make our family come first in any way that I could control.

We had made it work these past couple of years, but it

hadn't been easy. I had missed class presentations, baseball games, basketball games—you name it. On those occasions, I often hung up the phone after hearing about what I missed and thought, *What the hell am I doing here?* When I did get home from a trip, I was exhausted from the travel and emotionally drained. Yet I came home to a house where my husband had been mommy, daddy, nanny, and everything else for days on end and was ready to hand over the reins. My kids had had enough of my being away and would vie for my attention.

I also came home to a pile of work challenges. My constant BlackBerry checking had gotten so bad that my youngest son, James, had taken to calling my BlackBerry my "fourth son" because it was always with me at the table. (Just this past year, when Donald announced that he was going to fulfill a dream and attend law school, James raised his hand at the dinner table and said sarcastically, "Uh, do you guys remember you still have two children at home?")

My kids had permission to call me at any hour, but that did not ensure that the call would actually get through. Between the bad connections, the time delays, and the fact that young kids are not always great phone conversationalists, I often hung up dissatisfied and longing to have them in front of me. It was easier with Donald; he always had a number of things to talk to me about, and somehow we would muddle through the poor sound quality of overseas calls. I eventually agreed with my kids that in advance of our calls they would select one thing they did or thought about that day that I should know about. This way we had an agenda. It sounds silly, but it really helped.

The worst was when I called home to find that Donald or one of the kids had had a bad day. Especially at first, Donald was exhausted from work and not used to having to put dinner on the table or help the kids with their homework. Many a time, I felt terrible hearing the frustration in his voice, or the sadness or anxiety in one of my kids' voices, and not being able to hug them. I could feel in my bones the burden my job was placing on all of them.

Another painful part of travel was Jewish holidays. Donald is not Jewish, but we had agreed that we would raise our kids in the Jewish faith. That put the burden on me to make holidays and do other things to bring Judaism into our home. In my previous job working for a Jewish organization, I had gotten all the religious holidays off, so it hadn't been an issue. Now that I worked for an international organization, I often had to travel and attend critical meetings on Jewish holidays. Sure, I could go to a synagogue in Beijing, if I happened to be there, but I couldn't celebrate my faith with my kids.

I rarely talked in depth about these issues. I felt guilty if I complained about the demands of my home life and lacking in some way if I admitted my work life was overwhelming. One of my former employees who left for a corporate job remarked to me, "Caryl, your job is probably pretty lonely." And in fact it was. Navigating all of it was difficult, and whenever I felt like I had it all under control, something would happen to remind me I didn't.

I did try my best. I remained committed to a basic ground rule of my marriage to Donald—that we would allow each other to follow our dreams as long as we remembered that our biggest dream was a happy and healthy family. I wondered what my children would tell me one day twenty years from now when they looked back on this period. Would they only remember my absences, or would they have also noticed how hard I tried to balance it all? I hoped they would know that I never extended my trips any longer than my work demanded or that I refused to travel over weekends unless absolutely necessary. I hoped they would appreciate that my colleagues all poked fun at me because I took calls from my kids no matter where I was when the phone rang. Would they joke about the way ambassadors, congresswomen, or even the president of a major U.S. foundation had laughed when I interrupted our meetings for calls from my kids?

In many ways, the demands of my job were hardest on Lee. He had known life before I began to travel so much and could remember when I was PTA president and class mom. He had given up a lot, so I felt happy that I would have a chance during our trip to Brazil to make up for some of it. Most kids don't get a chance to visit a developing country, much less under the auspices of an organization like UNICEF. Lee would get a really deep, honest picture of the realities that exist around the world. This once-in-a-lifetime experience would broaden his horizons, allowing me to feel that I was providing him with the best possible education and passing along my cherished values of service and compassion. I would never really know if the sacrifices my family had made were worth it, but maybe after this trip I would at least feel that certain benefits had helped balance out the sacrifices—not just for me, but for all of us.

We arrived in Manaus late at night and checked right into our hotel. My staff had ordered pizza and we sat at a long table together as a group for the first time. I wondered what the group dynamics would be like. Would everyone get along? The hotel had an unusual free-form pool that looked like a miniature lake, and the kids needed to work off some energy, so we let them go swimming. Kids are great. While the moms sat and made polite chitchat, slowly getting to know one another, the kids bonded—led, I am happy to say, by Lee. They made up a game where they jumped off a wall by one side of the pool into the water. It was way past everyone's bedtime, but listening to their giggles, none of us had the heart to stop them. It was the perfect way to start the trip together, just having fun. Soon enough they'd meet with more serious challenges.

The next morning began with the discovery of huge iguanas—two or three feet long—their eyes bulging out of bizarre, scaled bodies. The hotel had a miniature zoo attached to it and the lizards ran loose. As we waited for breakfast, the kids were mesmerized by the creatures and went on an iguana hunt down the narrow, winding paths that ran across the zoo's heavily wooded, tropical grounds. At ten in the morning, it was time to call the kids in and get down to business.

"Do we have to come in?" they wailed.

"I'm afraid so," I replied. *Uh-oh,* I thought, *here comes the resistance I had feared.*

I led them into a meeting room where we had set up chairs in a circle. When everyone was settled, we went around formally introducing ourselves to one another and offering comments about why we had each chosen to participate. The mothers all delivered profound statements. "I've been a volunteer for ten years at UNICEF," one of them said, "and this is my chance to finally see what I've been helping to fund all these years. It's a chance for me to show my kids what's going on in the world." The kids, predictably, were less serious—and also less enthused. "I'm here because my mom thought it would be a good idea," one said. Glancing sideways at me,

Lee told the group, "I can't say I chose to come here. I was more informed that I was coming. And last night when I was packing, my mom wouldn't even let me take my Linkin Park T-shirt. Not cool." I also had noticed that most of the kids had brought electronic gadgets with them. Some even wore headphones.

The next hour was difficult. With the best of intentions, our UNICEF Brazil staff took sixty minutes to walk us through an overview of the country, most of which built upon information we'd already circulated to everyone. Still, I found it interesting to hear about the three Brazilian regions: the Amazon Platform (where we were visiting, home to 9 million children who largely lived in underdeveloped areas); the Brazilian Semi-arid Platform (home to 13 million children, 70 percent of whom lived in poverty); and the Urban Platform (where 16 million children and adolescents experienced the highest levels of violence). But the kids were yawning and staring out the window. In fact, a few had put their headsets back on in the middle of the presentation.

After the overview, RC came in to tell us his story. As he began to address our group through an interpreter, telling us his name and age, I thought, *I hope these children can last through another speaker.* I was in for a surprise. The kids remained rapt throughout his speech. We were all captivated. Looking down at the ground, RC went into more detail about what it was like to live with HIV.[1]

> I couldn't tell anyone, because even my best friends would have rejected me; they would have thought they would catch my disease. It was so lonely for me. My mother is HIV-positive, too, and I am seeing her get sicker and sicker, knowing that this could happen

to me someday. She is weak and there are times when she can't get out of her bed, and I have to take care of her. She can't cook for me or take me to school most of the time. But we don't talk about her being sick, either. I am HIV-positive because I was born with it. My mother kept saying how sorry she was to me that I was sick. I want to be strong for my mother. I don't want her to see when I'm sad or don't feel well.

My mother got really sick, so we took her to a clinic. They took care of her, and that's how I got tested and found out I was sick, too. They started me on drugs, but still my friends at home didn't know. I stayed to myself because I had all these feelings and nowhere to put them. I couldn't be myself with my friends, so it was easier to just be by myself.

RC's voice cracked as he spoke; you could tell he was re-counting his story before a group for the first time. Even the macho boys in our group had tears in their eyes.

Someone at UNICEF told me about this online chat room for kids like me. You could ask questions and share how you feel, and you could do it without any-body knowing who you were. I wanted to do this, but I didn't have a computer, and nobody I knew had a computer. I talked to the school where there might be a computer, but I was afraid to use the site in a public place. My mother understood and let me travel to the UNICEF office.

We hadn't begun to explore the Amazon River Basin yet, so we couldn't understand the environment RC lived in or how remote his village really was. Our children's mouths gaped, though, when they heard he didn't have ready access to a computer. They had taken it for granted that everyone was wired in, so essential was the technology to their lives. RC went on, visibly uncomfortable at what he was divulging: "In order to pay for the long trip to the UNICEF office on the bus, my mother had to skip meals, because we are very poor. It's tough because my mother is sick." Then his face lit up.

> We go anyhow, and it is amazing. I can go on a website and chat with other kids about the meds we're taking, have you told your friends, what do you tell them, how did they respond. It's incredible to talk to people who are experiencing what I'm experiencing. My mother and I both give up meals every other week so we can do this. It's the first time in my life that I can talk about my fears. I still feel guilty about my mother, but now I've started to become an activist, to talk to younger kids who are HIV-positive. I joined a movement on the web to change things here in Brazil. But I can still only go online a little bit every other week, because of the expense and how long it takes to get there.

By this time, the oddest thing had happened. Slowly the iPods and other gadgets were disappearing from the table and were discreetly being put away. There wasn't a headset in sight. Every child and mother was weeping. And when RC finished talking, we all stood and applauded him. But the best was yet to come. One of the women in our group had made a donation to our office in Brazil prior to the trip, and knowing that we'd be meeting with RC, UNICEF staff had purchased a computer for him. We presented him with this gift, and RC openly wept, breaking our stereotype of expected behavior for a boy in this macho culture.

Composing himself, he returned to the circle to address the group: "For many years, I have cried tears of sadness. But this is the first time that I've understood what tears of joy are. Please know that I cry from joy today. I don't know how to thank you enough, but I pledge to use the computer to mobilize as many young people as possible!"

Our children mobbed RC, giving him hugs and high-fives. This one child's story had done more to convey to our children why we were here than all the words we adults had thrown at them. Our children got it. As Lee and I locked eyes across the room, I sensed for the first time that I had done the right thing in bringing him here.

(I'm pleased to report that RC is now twenty years old and is living up to his promise. He currently leads the National Network of Adolescents and Youth Living with HIV/AIDS and is a powerful advocate for youth in Brazil and globally. He regularly meets with government leaders and is helping to shape policy in Brazil. He stands as living proof that if you invest in one, you can impact many.)

The next day, our Rio Negro adventure began. We rose early and walked to the river to board the boat we would live on as we traversed the river. The river here is massive, wider than the Hudson River back in New York, and dark with vegetation and fallen leaves. In Manaus, three major rivers actually come together to form the Amazon. We would be heading north, up the Rio Negro. I had no idea what our boat would look like; I had pictured everything from a dilapidated old vessel to a modern cruise ship. I was not the only one delighted to find a brand-new, sparkling white ship called the *Iana*, with three decks and a white-and-red flag flapping at its bow.

The kids ran right up the plank and onto the ship. They checked out the cabins, looked for lifeboats, and found the dining room. The cabins were tiny, each holding no more than a set of bunk beds and perhaps another cot-sized bed, but no dressers, desks, or closets. With their sterile white walls, floors, blankets, pillows, and sheets and a single overhead light reflecting off of everything, these cabins were a cross between a dorm room and the tiniest hospital room you could imagine, completely void of anything decorative or charming but functional and remarkably clean. Each was attached to a small bathroom with a shower, and each had a window that opened onto a walkway that wrapped around the ship's perimeter.

The crew gathered us in the dining room for an orientation, assigning us to our respective cabins and explaining the ship's basic rules. We learned that we were the only passengers aboard, and that the ship had only very recently been retrofitted, making us the first passengers to use it. The captain took us on a formal tour of the ship, pointing out that all of our cabins were abovedeck, so that everyone could see the countryside as we drifted. On the bridge, our kids eyed the massive wheel used to steer the ship and checked out the many maps and charts on the walls. A few of us took turns at the helm, while others snapped photos. My cabin was next to the bridge, the only one located in that area. I had expected it to look just like everyone else's, but it turned out I had been assigned the ship's only suite— spanning the ship's width and featuring a queen-sized bed and even a VCR—so I could hold meetings there with our donors.

As the boat left the riverbank, the kids went down to the dining area and began a game of Uno. It was amazing to watch them naturally assume their places around a table and begin a game. The youngest child on the trip was ten years old, the oldest seventeen, with a mix of boys and girls, yet all this seemed irrelevant. They were Americans in a foreign country, and this was enough to tie them together.

The Uno game continued over dinner, turning into an Uno championship tournament that lasted the entire trip. Meanwhile, the moms snuck out and found spots on the deck. We lay on our backs, marveling at the sky above as the boat pushed through pitch-black darkness on either side of us. The sheer plenitude and majesty of the stars captivated us, as did the shooting stars that streaked light in all directions. It didn't hurt that we were also sipping caipirinhas—drinks mixed by our Brazilian colleagues. As the alcohol flowed, everyone loosened up and the conversations got increasingly personal. Despite our diversity as a group, we bonded that night as women, mothers, and wives, talking about our kids, our husbands, our jobs, even menopause. There were serious moments and lots of laughs.

One by one, as they lost their rounds of Uno, the kids began to arrive. Lee burst into laughter seeing us all on the floor, eyes glued to the sky. But he found a place to squeeze in, just in time to see a huge orange ball appear on the horizon. At first we thought the jungle might be on fire. We were in the middle of nowhere and it was pitch black. But as the light grew bigger, we realized that it was the moon rising atop the jungle.

"Amazing," Lee whispered to me.

I looked over at him, thinking how lucky I was to have such a son and to have been given the chance to share this with him. "Sure is," I whispered back, patting his hand.

I'd never witnessed a "moonrise" before, but after that experience, I made sure I was on deck every night to see it again.

An hour later, we were tired and ready for bed, but we couldn't turn in, so beautiful was that sky. For me, a natural wonder such as this seemed to mitigate the pain I had felt listening to RC talk, reminding me that some things are bigger than the hell many children around the globe must suffer every day. Beauty certainly doesn't compensate for horror, but it does provide some respite, stirring compassion and generosity within us, and in this way, opening a pathway for hope.

Over the next few days, we visited villages up and down the river, tiny settlements consisting of a cluster of homes—usually ten or twenty, but never more than thirty—and an occasional community building, clinic, or school. In one larger village, the Brazilian kids taught our children local dances as well as a few defensive martial arts moves. At another village, we visited a modern community development center that held basic nutrition, child care, breast-feeding, prenatal, and postnatal classes for women. I was surprised by the conversation we had with our kids that first evening about the advantages of breast-feeding—a topic I had never considered talking with my son about before. The kids asked thoughtful questions, and they handled our answers without the expected giggles or awkwardness.

The next day, we exposed our children to a head-spinning array of experiences and realities. We visited a village where people lived in houses propped up on bamboo stilts, and where children had to take boats to get to school. We saw terrible poverty—families with little more than a bare hut to live in or a rickety paddle boat, children running around with no shoes and lacking access to potable running water. In another village, we came upon youth playing a game of kickball—something our children identified with immediately. In yet another village, we had the opportunity to watch children making all sorts of crafts, some of which they were allowed to sell in a small store.

This last stop became truly special when the Brazilian children invited our kids to try their own hands at carving. Supplied with a fist-sized block of wood and small hand tools, our kids began cutting and shaving to create shapes that would depict a simple dolphin. What looked easy when done by the Brazilian teens proved extremely difficult. Our teens were surprised how long it took to get a smooth curve, or how quickly a slip of the hand could ruin a piece of wood. It was fun to watch the kids teaching one another, crossing the language barriers, and celebrating when they finally succeeded in finishing the dolphins.

At another stop, we got a chance to give something back. One of the families with us had donated funds to build a playground at a school in Brazil. The gift had been made months earlier, and we were offered the privilege of participating in the ribbon-cutting ceremony that would open the playground for the first time. We arrived with UNICEF "recreation in a box" kits, which include items like basketballs, soccer balls, and Frisbees. It was an extremely hot day, and we huddled with our boxes under the only tree we could find, waiting for the ceremony to begin. The entire village had turned out; kids everywhere were eager to try out the new playground, while their moms were holding them back, trying to maintain some semblance of order.

After a few formal remarks, dignitaries cut the ribbon and the kids, many dressed in yellow and blue school uniforms, poured into the playground, squealing with delight as they swung in the swings, climbed the monkey bars, and slid down the slides. We distributed our kits, and the older kids immediately started a soccer game in one corner, while others tossed around Frisbees. Our kids jumped in and played alongside everyone else, completely forgetting the heat. The woman whose family had made the donation wept as she watched.

Back on the boat that evening, as we again lay on the deck watching the stars, one of the women seemed visibly upset. When I asked her what was wrong, she smiled and described an epiphany she had had. "Every one of our kids has a giant playground right in their backyard, and they never touch it. When we cut the ribbon today, it was like it was the greatest thing that had ever happened for those kids. How does that happen?"

Our children's minds were also opening by the minute. The next day, we visited a health clinic, and one of our boys asked where the waiting room was. "That's it," our UNICEF colleague said, pointing to long benches where women sat with children on their laps, waiting their turn under the hot sun. As we continued our walk through the clinic, the kids gawked as they watched the staff take notes with pens and file charts alphabetically in drawers. "Where are the computers?" a girl traveling with us asked. "There aren't any," we answered.

Our children learned even more while speaking with Brazilian mothers at the clinic. I asked one of the women to tell our kids, from beginning to end, how she came to be there sitting on the bench that day. She explained, "My baby did not seem right several days ago. She has been sleeping too much and not crying as much. She has had diarrhea, so I have brought her to the clinic."

"Why did you wait until today?" asked Lee, observing her baby, who was obviously ill. "Why not come sooner?"

The question seemed to confuse her. "Today is the day the doctor is here."

I further explained to our kids that a doctor could only come on certain days during the month. Even if there was a doctor available to make a diagnosis, more often than not patients lacked access to needed medications. I could see this was a lot for our children to take in. They were accustomed to seeing a doctor whenever it was necessary and to having access to whatever they needed to feel better.

That evening, we again returned to the boat, spread out on the deck, and discussed what we had seen. Curiously, our children—Lee included—had ceased to play any kind of electronic games since the speech given by RC. They were too taken by the intensity of experiencing a different culture and way of life. Instead, the Uno game continued, and they seemed to enjoy doing things together as one big gang. They also held long conversations among themselves. The only time a gadget came out was to play music for the whole group—not just through a single person's earphones—and only after the conversations had been completed. A few times, one of the kids played on a guitar he had brought with him. The crew on the boat reciprocated by playing Latin music for us, which we all enjoyed.

For Lee, the single most memorable moment of cultural exchange came on the last day of our river cruise, when we visited a school to deliver and stock books into a recently built library. After the time our children had spent in the smaller village schools, they were surprised to learn that in larger villages, some of the classrooms looked very much like theirs in the United States, minus the expensive technology. The class sizes here were larger than in most U.S. schools, with over forty kids per teacher, and textbooks were sparse, with several kids sharing each one. But the school here had concrete floors, ceilings, walls, and blackboards in every room, and the kids were dressed in Western clothes as at any New York City school.

We began our visit by dividing our kids into groups of two or three based upon their age. Lee and two other Americans went into a seventh-grade classroom to handle questions prepared by the Brazilian children: How old were our children? What were schools in America like? How long had our children been in Brazil? Most of the Brazilians spoke Portuguese and asked their questions through an interpreter. A few did speak English, and judging from their faces, quite a few of the others understood what our kids were saying even if they were not comfortable enough to speak in English. While both sides were initially shy, after the first few minutes the conversation seemed to roll out pretty easily.

Our children were asked if they had any questions of their own. "Does anyone like music?" Lee asked. A child in the back of the room stood up and shouted, "Linkin Park!"

Lee was floored; he looked like he'd seen a ghost. Linkin Park was his favorite band of all time. Here we were, in a school in the middle of the Amazon rain forest, and this child from an entirely different cultural background liked the exact same music. Lee's face lit up in sheer joy as he responded that he, too, loved Linkin Park. He shot me a look that said, "And you didn't let me bring the T-shirt!" All I could do was laugh.

Besides cultural exchange, we spent a good amount of time in the Amazon overcoming our fears about the local wild-life. One afternoon, while we were in a tributary of the Rio Negro, we set off in little canoes and went fishing for pira-nhas. The Amazon jungle is unlike anything I've ever seen. Because the water levels rise and fall, almost all of the trees grow directly out of the water and the branches hang very low. At times, we needed to duck under branches as we wove into passageways so narrow I didn't think our boats would fit. We cut one corner a little too close, and as one of the kids grabbed a branch to keep it from hitting her face, she was smacked by another, smaller one laden with thorns. Luckily, one of the moms was a nurse and had come along for this exact reason. She helped tweeze out the thorns, and the young girl was a real trooper. We were in the Amazon, and we were going to do this!

We arrived at the spot our guide had chosen for fishing, finding a narrow pool framed by a ceiling of thick, overhang-ing trees. Bees swarmed everywhere, putting our children on edge, but our guide didn't understand what they were afraid of. Bees were simply a part of his everyday life, nothing out of the ordinary. Our guide proceeded to get out a fishing line and demonstrated how to attach it to sticks. Now I was ner-vous. I had never actually seen real piranhas. Was this a good idea? Was it dangerous? To their credit, other moms with us chucked their lines into the water and went for it. Soon all of us were fishing, flapping our lines to attract the fish. Some-one got a bite, and after a pause for dramatic effect, the fish popped out of the water. It did have teeth, and our guide told us that they have been known to pick their prey clean in only a few hours, hard to believe when the fish we saw was only five inches long.

As the sun was moving lower in the sky, we put our make-shift rods away and left the fishing area. The guide suggested we continue along the river a bit longer—this part of the river was surrounded by lush trees and the sunset would be beautiful. We took a vote and found the group evenly split. Glancing at the kids' faces, I could see that a few were afraid of being out in these small boats after dark, but that they were embarrassed to say so. I made an executive decision that we would return, prompting expressions of relief.

Part of the group did get a night out on the river, though. All of the kids and a few moms went "alligator hunting." They left after dark, again in small boats, and floated up a small tributary into an area of dense, almost impenetrable jungle. I didn't go on this expedition, but as Lee and others recounted, you could hear creatures in the trees and the sounds of animals moving about in the distance. The group got quieter as they moved farther into the darkness. Some of the adults whispered things like "It was a dark and stormy night, the river was *angry* that night" in jest to break the mood. Suddenly, the guide stood up in the boat and shined a flashlight in the water. With no notice, he plunged into the water.

The kids were terrified, not knowing where he had gone, since the water was too murky to see into. Even the adults were on edge, remembering the piranhas teeming in this area. Each person silently counted the seconds. Finally, the guide reemerged with a small alligator, which he dragged into the boat. The kids moved as far away from it as they could, scared out of their minds. Soon they realized that the danger was not as great as they had imagined. "Hunting for alligators" became the story of the trip, the size of the alligator and the darkness of the night both greatly embellished in its telling.

On another afternoon, almost all of us ended up in the water. We were invited to swim with pink dolphins in a narrow section where the sea mixes with the river, raising the water's salt content. Piranhas and alligators can't live here, but dolphins thrive. I had dreamed of swimming with dolphins for some time, picturing myself gliding through the water and holding on to a fin in an almost ethereal way. On this day, faced with actually diving into a murky, brown river, I almost changed my mind. There is so much vegetation in the jungle, not to mention bugs, spiders, snakes, beetles, birds, and fish, that it truly feels like the center of the living world. And I was about to jump in.

I knew I needed to suck it up and show I wasn't afraid, so I finally did. The water was icy cold. The dolphins were only about three feet long and they swam so deep that we couldn't see them at first. In fact, I couldn't see my hand six inches below the surface. Then the dolphins started to bump into our legs and stomachs. You could tell their locations by the screams of the group. We all treaded water with our life jackets and waited for contact. I was terrified, but I hung in there. By the time the dolphins surfaced, we had each been bumped, and on occasion, the dolphins barreled out of the water and splashed back down next to us. I remember thinking that if we had been in the United States, we would have had to sign a waiver three pages long to take part in an activity like this. But here in the Amazon, anything was game. It was far from the ethereal experience I had imagined, but I was satisfied with myself for joining in.

On our last night in Brazil, we gathered together as a group and debriefed about all we had seen on the trip. Lee talked about the kid who yelled out "Linkin Park!" and how surprised he had been: "I expected to see that kids were different in Brazil, but I didn't know that life was so tough and sad. It was more different than I expected, the poverty was far greater. I can't imagine living RC's life down here. But I also didn't expect I'd find a kid thousands of miles away who speaks a different language but likes the same music. For some reason, that makes me feel connected." Many of the other children in our group nodded in agreement. Another child remarked: "The kids we met along the river looked like some of the friends we have at home, but their day-to-day lives are so different. Even when they speak English, there are huge differences between how we live at home and how they live." A number of the children stated their intention to get involved in social action. One girl said, "I can't pretend any longer that bad stuff isn't happening around the world." As I listened, all I could think was, *I know exactly how you feel.*

When we arrived back in New York and settled into our normal lives, I watched Lee closely. I was wondering if the emotions he brought back from Brazil would dissipate, taking his new awareness of the world with them. During the first few days, we discussed ways we could alter our lives to express more appreciation for the things we usually take for granted. We smiled at one another as we made sure all the lights were turned out when everyone left a room, or when we turned off the water instead of letting it run while we brushed our teeth. I was no longer the only one in our home who had seen that for many children around the world, electricity and running water are unimaginable luxuries.

A number of kids who had gone on the trip spent time talking to their classes at school about their experiences; they also found ways to get involved and engaged in our agenda. A few joined Lee in participating in a walk to raise money to make good, clean drinking water accessible to children in places where it wasn't already. I heard from several of the mothers that the trip seemed to have changed their children, making them more socially conscious and committed to charitable projects. One child helped found a UNICEF club in his school that raised money for kids in various countries. Another girl donated her sweet-sixteen money because of what she had seen in Brazil.

On a personal level, Lee and I had shared an adventure— one that had brought both giggles and tears and that would stay with us for the rest of our lives. He had a chance to get a better idea of what Mom does at work, and I had a chance to see what I did through his eyes. RC's presentation had an impact on us both. Watching Lee absorb all that RC had to say made me realize how much my son had grown and how great his ability to empathize was. Lee had not only understood RC's challenges; he had also appreciated the great integrity RC projected. I got a glimpse of the man Lee would one day grow into.

I also had some great professional moments as I watched children experience epiphanies, learning what the world is really like. Sure, I had seen far worse examples of poverty in other places, but our children had not. In Brazil, they discovered firsthand the impact that humanitarian workers on the ground can have. And they experienced how something ordinary to them, such as a computer, can mean the world to someone else.

Most of all, the trip confirmed for me the great responsibility we as parents have to teach our children about diversity and to help them fit into the global village our world has become. We have to stretch ourselves to ensure that our children become openminded as well as think from a global perspective—they should become empathetic and understanding of local cultural traditions.

I came away from this trip recognizing how lucky I was to be able to allow Lee this opportunity as well as how important it would be to do more in the weeks, months, and years ahead. We may not have to cross an ocean to experience diversity or hone our global skills, but expansion of our awareness doesn't happen unless we as parents take responsibility.

In my previous book, *Hate Hurts,* my coauthor and I offered suggestions that parents can use to help their kids talk about, understand, and embrace our differences. We believed then, and I still believe, that prejudice is learned, and that we can unlearn it or even prevent the learning from taking place to begin with. As parents, we send subtle messages all of the time. We need to examine those messages and consider how they are being received.

Many years ago, a speaker I heard began his talk by asking the audience to fill in the blank of his next sentence. He began "The moon is made of _____." The crowd almost unanimously yelled out "Cheese." We all giggled. He then pointed out that at some point in our childhood, someone had relayed this fact and today, even though we know it to be false, we still answer, "Cheese." And so it is with stereotypes, bigotry, and prejudice. We receive these messages as children and they stay with us. Unless we consciously send a message to our kids that differences can enhance us, we may inadvertently close them off to any number of enriching opportunities.

As parents, we can commit to consciously installing positive messages about differences and global cultures. Research your community for museums, exhibits, or programs that educate your children about the peoples of the world. Ask friends and other caregivers to share stories and traditions. Create a family project in which your children do a bit of research on a particular culture, culminating in an evening of foods and games from that culture. Scour your cable box for television channels that offer English-language programming from other cultures.

Our interactions with our kids can play a huge role, too. Talk openly about global realities and cultural differences. Build your children's appreciation for the contributions of all cultures by telling them where the things they enjoy come from. A teenager who loves hip-hop might be fascinated to learn that it stems from the African oral and drum tradition. A toddler who will only eat McDonald's fries might gain broader insight by learning its origins in French cuisine. A preteen who obsesses about her nails can discover that she is actually practicing an ancient Asian art of body decoration. Knowing that we all draw on a wide range of cultures can help keep our children from thinking that their particular cultural niche is all-encompassing, and that other cultures are strange. That in turn forms the basis for caring about other people and how they are living around the world.[2]

It's important to grasp opportunities to teach our children about global issues when they arise. After the encounter with RC, I didn't simply let our memory of it drift away; rather, I tried on many occasions to discuss with Lee different dimensions of the experience. This led us over time to probe deeper into the lives of kids in other cultural settings. It's one thing for a child to understand that the world is a big place filled with diversity, another thing to really appreciate all the implications and nuances. As a parent, I had the ability to steer Lee's thinking and create an ongoing dialogue that over time would nourish a meaningful commitment to service.

Many cultures share similar stories and customs as ways of teaching children. Let your children know about these similarities as you discover them. There is a story from both Jewish and African culture that gives a wonderful description of heaven and hell, and that also offers a lesson in how we should treat one another. To this day, it remains one of my favorite stories. Here is my recollection of the version I learned in a workshop I took many years ago.

The Chasidic Jews describe heaven and hell as the same basic scene. Hell consists of a very, very, very long table surrounded by many, many chairs. In each chair sits a person who is very, very hungry, almost starving. In the middle of the table sits a pot of the most delicious, nutritious soup. And the people are salivating from the aroma—anticipating the taste. Each person is given a long-handled spoon that they use to reach into the pot. They turn their spoons around to eat, but the handles are so long that they hit their faces and the soup spills. Thus, hell is one continuous seeking for fulfillment without ever getting it. In heaven, you have the same scene. With one major difference. Remember those long-handled spoons? Well, here instead of dipping into the pots and turning their spoons around, hitting their faces, and spilling the soup, the people at the table dip into the pot and then reach across the table and feed one another.

We must help our kids—and ourselves—to learn how to dip into our own pots, reach across our cultures, and feed one another, metaphorically as well as literally.

5. THE WHITE SHIRTS OF HAITI

Haiti, January–October 2010

Despite everything, I believe that people are really good at heart.

—ANNE FRANK

PEOPLE OFTEN RELIVE over and over those last few moments before a disaster hits. We ponder the incomprehensible suddenness with which our sense of normalcy was taken from us, and we wonder whether we somehow missed the signals that something terrible was about to take place. I look back in this way on January 12, 2010, the day an earthquake registering 7.0 on the Richter scale struck just outside the Haitian capital of Port-au-Prince.

I was sitting in my office late in the day, wrapping up a report I was writing, when my screen lit up with emails about the quake. I turned on CNN and consulted the ribbon of information scrolling across the bottom of the screen. The quake had occurred only minutes ago, and little information was available. I asked my staff to contact UNICEF's Emergency Operations Center in New York City to see what they knew. The center, established under Carol Bellamy's

123

leadership of UNICEF, tracks indicators of possible trouble around the world—weather patterns, seismic shifts, conflict escalations, even Internet chatter. It serves as a repository of information as disasters unfold, with UNICEF staff on the ground and others reporting what they are seeing and experiencing firsthand. In this case, the center had only sketchy information, since the quake destroyed United Nations facilities in Haiti.

The entire mood on our floor changed as word of the earthquake spread from office to office. Just a moment earlier, people had been telling jokes in the halls, getting ready to head home, but now there was eerie silence. Many of my colleagues had visited Haiti over the years, and some even had close friends working there. Were they okay? What happened to their families? How long would it be before we knew?

As horrified and worried as we were, we understood that we couldn't afford to let our emotions paralyze us. News networks were already predicting a major humanitarian disaster, which meant that UNICEF and other agencies would be working hard to put together an in-depth rescue, recovery, and rebuilding response for the people of Haiti. We at the U.S. Fund for UNICEF would need to get the United States to support those efforts—and do it quickly.

We got to work within minutes. Our internal emergency response team convened immediately. Our senior management team met in my office, and we began to identify organizations and individuals we could call upon to support our efforts. We divided the list into those whom we could approach for financial support, those who could help us engage others, and those who fit both categories. We discussed what we would say to the American public and assigned our communications team to mount both a short-term and long-term strategy. Then the real work began, reaching out to all possible sources of support.

My first assignment: seek monies from something called the Mercury Fund. Several years earlier, under my predecessor's leadership, thanks to a generous donor our organization had established this special fund for use during extraordinary emergencies, when cash is short and demands for resources high. Unlike other, more bureaucratic funding sources, the Mercury Fund requires the approval of only two board members, allowing for quick and easy access. Phone calls and emails go to all four board members, but once two of the four agree that a request corresponds with the fund's mandate, dollars are immediately released, usually within twenty-four hours of the emergency. As the fourth member of the Mercury Fund board, I reached out to the other three. Approval was unanimous, and our first tranche of money was sent.

Next we called our generous friends at the National Basketball Association, seeking their financial support and also help from NBA players in engaging the public. We also reached out to our friends at 1199 SEIU, the United Healthcare Workers Union, an organization with many Haitian members, and other American organizations with roots or interests in Haiti. Less than a year earlier, we had convened a meeting of representatives from organizations interested in Haiti so as to build relationships we could count on. Our goal had been to find ways to work together that might help us all to maximize support for the people of Haiti, especially during the harsh hurricane season each year. Good thing we did—the friendships formed would now serve Haiti in ways far more profound than any of us could have anticipated.

Our communications team began to disseminate our pleas

on behalf of Haiti's earthquake survivors, and they also collected information by the minute from our colleagues on the
ground through personal phone calls and official UN channels. The picture became somewhat clearer over the next
several days, and it was bleak indeed. Wracked by longstanding political instability, this country of 9.9 million was already
listed as the poorest in the Western Hemisphere, ranked
among the lowest of all countries in human development.
One-third of Haiti's children were malnourished, and the
government was long considered unstable. Now a bad situation had become inestimably worse. The international airport
at Port-au-Prince was inoperable. The country's few hospitals
had crumbled to the ground or been severely damaged, and
most major and minor roads in the vicinity of Port-au-Prince
and other cities were damaged and choked with debris. Mu-
nicipal buildings in the capital were damaged or destroyed,
and the offices of international organizations like the World
Bank and the United Nations Stabilization Mission were
gone. Thousands of people were sleeping in the streets, because even the best-built homes had been eviscerated. Amidst
all the chaos, untold numbers of children were wandering
about, separated from their families, or even worse, left orphaned as a result of the quake.

To make matters worse, the path to an effective international response was not clear. Normally, the UN hierarchy
organizes agencies, countries, and private organizations wishing to help in an emergency. UN leadership in a given country coordinates the UN agencies (such as UNICEF) using
a system that allows different agencies to take the lead on
various aspects of the plan. In Haiti, UN representatives were
also victims of the quake—some dead, others injured, many
traumatized. A response plan existed, but obstacles like the

lack of telephones made implementation difficult. People on the ground did what they had been trained to do, but it took longer than usual to pass on information, to account for staff, to assess the damage and put resources in place. Meanwhile, thousands of well-meaning organizations, governments, and individuals from around the world were descending on Haiti trying to help. Confusion on the ground was something we would have to contend with over the next week as we tried to support efforts to help Haiti's children.

Phone calls coming into our office offered some indication of the dire situation. Often during humanitarian crises, we receive appeals for help from other organizations or governments. Now we were being contacted directly by individuals in Haiti who knew about UNICEF and expressed desperate need. One man from an orphanage emailed saying he had a couple of hundred children on his hands with no food or water. Others emailed saying they were trapped in unstable buildings and required rescue. As my staff read these pleas aloud, I stared at the cup of tea and half-eaten sandwich on my desk. What do you say to someone trapped in a space, thousands of miles away, too far to run to, too far to directly help? We passed these calls to the appropriate people, feeling grateful that we were at least doing our jobs. I had nightmares for weeks, seeing the orphans without food, the woman trapped under a beam, the parents who could not locate their children.

Traditionally, the U.S. Fund's relief efforts focus on raising cash, not material goods. Because of how difficult it is to transport material goods to a disaster scene, it's normally far cheaper and easier to source new items locally. But Haiti didn't only need money—it needed food, medicine, and supplies. The day after the quake, I received a call from the head of UNICEF's child protection programs, Dr. Susan Bissell. She explained that many Haitian children did not have birth certificates and were not registered with the government in any way. This made it impossible for aid workers already on the ground to know which children belonged to which parents, or who to unite with whom, or which adult was a relative and thus had the right to make decisions for children who had lost parents in the quake. A registry of remaining children had to be created as quickly as possible, requiring items such as digital cameras and hospital bracelets. Could I help?

I went to my local camera store and bought them out of cameras. A friend and I moved on to other camera stores, snatching up as many as we could. Hospital bracelets proved harder to find. I worked the phone trying to find a store that sold them, and kept striking out. Finally I called a friend who works as a nurse in the emergency room of a Bronx hospital. She and another nurse drove across New York City to area hospitals, begging, borrowing, and stealing as many bracelets as they could, dropping them on my front porch sometime after midnight. Going through the bracelets, I found the manufacturer's name and put in a call to the CEO. He sent me thousands more the next day.

Over the next few weeks, I worked intensely with donors to raise money for relief efforts, and I also found my love for my own country strengthening. Americans wanted so badly to help, and many went the extra mile, reaching deep into their wallets and pocketbooks in an outpouring of heartfelt support for the people of Haiti. The National Basketball Association, the NBA Players Association, and Major League Baseball each gave $1 million to fund emergency relief, as did 1199 SEIU. Jefferies & Company donated a day of their trading fees, totaling $1 million. I cried each time another major gift came to the table and also upon reading heartfelt letters from American children who sent us their allowance, birthday money, or dollars raised selling cupcakes and lemonade. Thousands of Americans sent in checks, and no matter what the size, the sentiment was the same: "We are so fortunate here that we will share with our Haitian brothers and sisters."

United Parcel Service (UPS) found a different way to contribute, helping us fulfill a very unusual but critical request from UNICEF's Emergency Operations Center. A few days after the earthquake, I was huddling with my senior management team when an urgent call came in from Louis-Georges Arsenault. I barely knew Louis-Georges at the time, but I understood his role as director of the center well enough to realize that if he said it was urgent, it was urgent. I asked our management team to wait and took the call. In his very French accent, and with all of the politeness he could muster, Louis-Georges wondered if the U.S. Fund could help UNICEF amass a list of toiletries and other necessities to create survival packages. These packages would in turn be distributed to Haitian children who had been separated from their families or orphaned by the earthquake.

Although we normally didn't solicit goods, the sheer number of children at risk in this situation called for an exception. I relayed the request to my team, and they all eagerly nodded yes. Louis-Georges rattled off a list of fourteen different items we needed to collect, including toothbrushes, soap, flip-flops, shampoo, bed mats, and blankets. My team members, who got the gist of the conversation, shot me concerned looks. How would we get this stuff together?

I brushed them off. "Sure, Louis-Georges, we can do that,

no problem. How many of each item are we looking for? A couple hundred?"

His response floored me. "Uh, try fifty thousand of each. And there's more to it than just collecting them. Once you've found all the items, you need to get them to a place where you can unpack them and then repack them into individual kits containing one of each item. Then you need to place the kits in boxes that are not too heavy to be carried by one person. The roads are not accessible, and even if they were, we do not have trucks to load them into. Once the boxes arrive in Haiti, they will be primarily transferred by hand." Louis-Georges let these facts settle in my mind before he quietly added: "And Caryl, this has to be accomplished in seventy-two hours if we are to get them into Haiti using the transportation at our disposal. Can you do that?"

My heart thumped in my chest. When I repeated these specifics to my team members, they all looked like they were about to kill me. "Absolutely, Louis-Georges," I said. "Of course we can. We'll get right on it."

You know the expression, "Fake it until you make it"? After I hung up, we sat there in shock, wondering what to do. I knew about raising money and running organizations, but never had I put together a relief response like this. I had no idea what it would take. Where would I get the items? Do we buy them or have them donated? If we buy them, what is a reasonable price? How do I get them to a single location? Where was that location? How large did that location need to be? How many people did I need to help unpack and re-pack the items? Where would I get the packing materials? With only seventy-two hours to work with, I needed to get every part of this perfectly right.

The senior management team and I decided to divide and

conquer, each of us taking responsibility for amassing certain items. Our corporate outreach team kicked into action, requesting help from the major corporations that produced some of these products. Our fundraisers reached out to individuals who held leadership positions anywhere that might help us get hold of components for the kit. With each phone call, more and more people joined our efforts, getting their own networks involved.

I personally took responsibility for the logistics—consolidating the items at one location and shipping them to Haiti. I got on the phone right away with our good friends at UPS: president of UPS International, Dan Brutto, and Ed Martinez, head of the company's charitable arm, the UPS Foundation. "Help!" I said. "You guys are the logistics experts. What do I do? We only have three days to make this happen."

Not four hours later, a UPS team from one of the company's local facilities was sitting in my office. Within twenty-four hours, UNICEF logistics experts from Copenhagen had arrived. Working swiftly like the professionals they are, they mapped out a plan. Over the next forty-eight hours, trucks would bring pallets of goods we collected to a warehouse in New Jersey. A team of volunteers would then sort through the goods, unpack the pallets, and repack them into small kits, which we would fly down to Miami for shipment to Haiti.

The next forty-eight hours were wild. Our team ran around frantically, making calls and reporting results. People ran into my office shouting, "I found half of the toothbrushes!" or "I've got twenty thousand bars of soap!" We learned that even with the best of intentions, no one had fifty thousand pieces of any one item we needed on hand and ready to donate. We would need to source each item from a number of donors and locations. Still, our partners came through. Henkel Consumer Goods donated soap, and Colgate-Palmolive donated toothbrushes, toothpaste, and soap, jumping through hoops to expedite shipping so the products arrived within forty-eight hours, a major feat.

One item on the list—bed mats—gave us more trouble. None of us really knew for sure what bed mats were, much less where to get them. One of the secretaries in our offices mentioned that she had had to buy her daughter a bed mat for naptime at nursery school. "Great," I screamed, "where did you buy it?" She named a small store in Chinatown. I called the store and spoke with a woman whose lack of proficiency in English made the conversation quite difficult. Somehow, the woman understood what I was asking and joined our team, hunting down a source for us and securing a donation.

The next question that arose for me was: how could we get volunteers in a hurry to do the unpacking and repacking? I put in a plea to UNICEF headquarters and to everyone in our New York office. The work would take place on a Saturday; all I had to offer volunteers was a free T-shirt and a bus ride to the New Jersey warehouse UPS had made available to us. Would enough people step up and help?

That Saturday, I rose at 4:00 a.m. and drove to New Jersey from my house in nearby Queens, New York. I had wanted to arrive at the warehouse early so as to greet and thank the volunteers as they stepped off the bus. Boy, was I in for a surprise. I pulled up at the warehouse to find more than a hundred volunteers from UPS already present on this freezing cold January morning, all wearing the company's iconic brown shirts and applauding me for the work the U.S. Fund was doing on behalf of Haiti's children. I was so moved at their compassion and devotion. Then a bus pulled up and a mix of people from the greater UNICEF family—from senior management all the way down to receptionists—got off, all wearing blue UNICEF shirts. Standing at the door to the bus, I greeted each one with a hug. As the UNICEF people saw their UPS colleagues, many of them burst into tears. We stood there hugging each other and basking in the knowledge that people really are kind. It was an experience I'll never forget.

Working at huge tables set up in the warehouse, we spent hours assembling the raw goods into kits, talking joyously with others nearby, many of whom we didn't know. Some volunteers had brought their children, and they ran around the warehouse, adding to the positive energy. By the end of the day, we were exhausted, but all the trucks had been loaded and sent to a UPS plane waiting at New York City's LaGuardia Airport for shipment to Miami. This completed what we had come to call Operation Stack and Pack. To this day, I am still amazed that all of us and numerous partners were able to work together to do the impossible on behalf of people none of us had ever met. Can you imagine what something like a blanket or a toothbrush can mean to a small child who has just lost everything? As Nelson Mandela once said, "It always seems impossible until it is done."

Reflecting back on this period, I am especially proud of the effort my own team made. For many weeks after the quake, my colleagues worked around the clock. Our celebrity team, telemarketing team, and fundraisers joined forces around a telethon called "Hope for Haiti Now" that raised money for a variety of relief efforts, including UNICEF.

Our direct-marketing team strategized about the correct email to send to donors to encourage them to give. Teams across our organization worked with other agencies and celebrities to coordinate a response. Meanwhile, we did everything we could to find out what happened to the UNICEF team on the ground in Haiti, wanting to be sure that everyone was okay.

It turned out that none of our workers were killed, although many had lost family members, homes, and cars. Their stories, when we learned them, were not merely sad but inspiring. One of our Haitian drivers lost three of his children, sheltered his wife and remaining children at the staff compound, and yet he still showed up for work. His supervisors told him he could go home, but he told them that he had to stay. "There is nothing more I can do for my wife and kids, but I can do something for my people. You have to let me stay."

One night, I came in at 1:00 a.m. with doughnuts and coffee for everyone as a way to say thanks. I found the phone bank fully staffed in service to the telethon and other senior leaders there lending a hand. Nobody was complaining. Everybody had come in simply because they cared. I was so proud to find them there and humbled by their commitment. As the leader of the organization, this was one of those moments when I reflected on how privileged I was to work with such amazing people.

I went to Haiti twice in 2010, the first time three weeks after the quake, the second time about ten months later. What I remember most from these trips aren't the scenes of devastation, as searing as they were, but the hope and belief in the future shown by the Haitian people. I was seasoned enough to know that children are children wherever you go, jumping on your lap, playing, laughing. Yet I found it heartening—deeply inspiring—to see this hold true even in a place like Haiti, where a single catastrophic event had, in an instant, ended lives and turned an entire society upside down. Like RC in Brazil, or the children in Darfur's internally displaced persons camps, the children of Haiti revealed themselves not merely as victims or people to be pitied but powerful makers of their own destiny, simply because they had decided to hang on and remain hopeful. Their example of strength affirmed for me an important life lesson: the human spirit perseveres even when we're most tempted to think its light has gone out.

I initially visited Haiti because our ongoing fundraising operations demanded it. After Operation Stack and Pack, I conducted more media interviews than I could count during which I tried to make everyday Americans aware of the horrible situation on the ground. The only way to really report on the situation with the maximum amount of authenticity and emotion was to see it with my own eyes. As soon as the earthquake happened, I wanted to travel to the country, but that had been impossible—commercial airlines were not flying in or out, and conditions were too unstable to ensure my safety. About three weeks after the quake, it was finally possible to organize a few days in the country with the help of the United Nations, so I eagerly signed up.

I don't mean to imply that I wasn't nervous about the trip. I absolutely was! Not only was Haiti still experiencing aftershocks; there were no hotels operating in the country, so I would have to sleep in a tent with other aid workers—something I hadn't done in twenty-five years. I also worried about violence in Haiti. Far from peaceful before the quake, the country had seen its share of violence since, and I had no idea if I would be safe sleeping outdoors in a tent. Where would I get clean food and water? Although I had traveled in some pretty dicey areas, I hadn't experienced emergency conditions before, and I wasn't sure I was comfortable with the idea.

I went anyway, accompanied by my colleague Lisa Szarkowski; we found seats on the first commercial flight into Port-au-Prince from the United States. The flight was unforgettable. Half the passengers were aid workers from a variety of organizations, some large, well-established, international aid groups and some newly formed, small, local groups. The rest were Haitians who had either been out of the country at the time of the disaster or who lived in the United States and were returning to visit their relatives. As the island of Hispaniola (shared by Haiti and the Dominican Republic) came into view, the plane grew quiet. We flew over Port-au-Prince and you could immediately see the devastation. This entire city of approximately 2.3 million people was flattened—not just a few blocks here or there, but the entire city. Passengers on the plane wept. The pilot got on the loudspeaker and offered a message: "To those going home, our prayers are with you, and to those who are coming to help, our heartfelt thanks."

We taxied down the tarmac to the half-ruined terminal. Inside, we found people running here and there, the airport staff throwing bags haphazardly into a large room. Throngs of Haitian children ran up to passengers, offering to carry their bags for a dollar. It was unbearably hot. It took us a while, but Lisa and I finally found our UNICEF Haiti colleagues, located our bags, and made our way to a white UNICEF jeep for the one-mile ride to the campsite.

With so many roads destroyed, the traffic was intense, and that one-mile trip took us a full hour. We couldn't see much, since the road didn't go through the city's heart. The campsite occupied the site of a former military base, and I was somewhat relieved to see that we had to pass through very tight security to get inside. This relief was short-lived. During a security briefing, they advised us not to go out at night, since many police and other authorities had been killed in the earthquake. They also told us that we needed to be prepared in case of further aftershocks. Not exactly the kind of information that would alleviate my anxiety.

The camp was immense—hundreds, maybe thousands, of acres. As we drove to an area occupied by UNICEF, I saw rows of tents and also thousands of people, including soldiers wearing the uniforms of national militaries: French, Spanish, Russian, British, and various Arab countries. These soldiers all were walking around, going about their business. Their countries of origin seemed wonderfully irrelevant. Everyone was focused on one goal: helping the people of Haiti.

Lisa and I arrived at the UNICEF area and claimed a spot to later pitch our tent. Amidst the UNICEF tents and surrounded by a few small prefabricated containers, a larger tent served as a makeshift office. Staff were sleeping in the containers, since they were just about the only places equipped with power and air-conditioning. We learned to our dismay that there were precisely two toilets and two showers for the three hundred of us in the area. Still, I felt happy to be surrounded with colleagues from around the world. Within a few minutes, I ran into someone I knew from Canada, another person from the United States, a third from a trip I had taken to Vietnam. *Okay,* I thought to myself, *this isn't as scary as I thought.*

We got back into our jeep, and a UNICEF driver took us outside the camp for an initial look at the damage. Looking out my window, I saw dilapidated houses and completely leveled buildings—rubble rising up everywhere. On every inch of open ground, people had erected tents, since their homes were completely destroyed or, at best, uninhabitable. The tents filled the landscape; on the roads, in the medians, everywhere. Entire streets were impassable. The horror of the earthquake started to sink in as we rolled along.

So, too, was an impression of UNICEF's vital work here. We were stuck in traffic when a large UNICEF water tanker truck pulled up next to us. Since the city infrastructure wasn't working, UNICEF was trucking in clean water to inhabitants of tent cities and remote areas. I got out, ran up to the truck, and talked to the driver, a young, recently hired Haitian man. He seemed so proud to be working for UNICEF. He didn't speak fluent English (and I didn't speak Creole or French, the languages spoken by most Haitians), but we could communicate well enough. He told me he had lost his home in the earthquake, but that his wife and child were still alive, and he was using his salary from this job to feed them. As we spoke, people passing the truck in other cars honked and gave us a thumbs-up, recognizing us for our UNICEF shirts and what we were doing for their country. By the time I climbed back into my jeep, I, too, was beaming with pride.

We went back to camp to get ourselves settled and ready for dinner. Lisa and I realized that neither of us New York girls had any idea how to pitch a tent. We tried to follow the directions, but we couldn't get it up, and as darkness fell, we laughed hysterically at our own ineptitude. Eventually we succeeded. Moving our supplies inside, we went to join thousands of others having dinner in the camp's large commissary. "Oh, I forgot something," Lisa said, so we went back. Turned out she had left the flap to our tent open, thinking that the fresh air would cool things down. Every bug in the greater Port-au-Prince metropolitan area seemed to have found our tent a welcome respite.

I dreaded the thought of sleeping amidst what I feared might be disease-ridden mosquitoes. Lisa and I sprayed every inch of our bodies as well as the tent. Even so, I was so agitated that I couldn't sleep that night. It was extremely hot out, but I insisted on staying in my sleeping bag, thinking that the fabric would protect me from being eaten alive. I had always been terribly afraid of bugs; now the specter of an early death hung over me as buzzing filled my ears. I had my computer with me, and, as in Mozambique, I tried watching a television show I had downloaded to help me fall asleep. Even that didn't work.

On the plus side, I found right away that living in a disaster zone did have its pleasures. Eating dinner in the commissary, I enjoyed the fellowship and camaraderie of hundreds of colleagues. It felt a bit like living in an episode of the TV show *MASH*: everyone around me had spent their day seeing horrific things, and now that they were taking a break, they engaged in normal chitchat and told macabre jokes, the horror lingering just under the surface. "Did you hear how the Yankees did last night?" someone would say just after a fellow diner had recounted pulling people out of the rubble.

The next day, we toured more of Port-au-Prince and began talking to people to get a sense of what had happened. Driving through pop-up tent cities and former commercial districts to the middle of the capital, we saw rubble everywhere, collapsed buildings, children sitting on the street playing, fallen electrical wires and telephone poles, masses of people lingering and walking about. The formerly magnificent presidential palace was missing walls. In the downtown area, the main cathedral—a huge, white, pristine building—now stood in ruins, cracks running along its foundation, its steeple simply gone.

Somehow, the cross on the steeple hadn't been damaged, and the faithful had dragged it across the street and leaned it against a retaining wall. It was one of the most stunning and spiritual things I had ever seen. A woman of about my age was standing nearby and her children were sitting under the cross. The woman was angry and hungry and begging us for help. At the same time, she held strongly to her faith. When she calmed enough for us to interview her, she proclaimed, "G-d will protect me!" I wondered if my own belief in G-d would have persisted as strongly.

Next we went to a soccer stadium. Thousands of people were living there, the tents so densely packed that you could barely walk among them. The country staff guiding us related that the area was unsafe, with no security or running water. The stench of sewage and rot was overwhelming. As we talked to people, we found that special tents had been set up in the middle of the stadium, places where women who had just given birth could come to learn how to breast-feed and to receive support. We visited one of these tents and played with the babies. A little girl of about three or four approached me. "Do you want to see where I brush my teeth?"

I said I did, and she led me to the sole source of running water for all these thousands of people, a fire hydrant located right outside the stadium. Throngs of women were standing about, bathing their children in the spray. A woman in her seventies was taking a shower in public, absolutely naked.

Knowing that most Haitians are religious and therefore practice modesty, I couldn't imagine how desperate this woman must have been to suffer such public indignity. She clearly had no choice: the privacy that I took for granted in New York City was an unaffordable luxury here.

Continuing our tour, Lisa and I visited an all-girls orphanage whose buildings had been entirely destroyed and whose orphans were living in makeshift tents. It was terribly hot, and the nuns who were running the place were obviously exhausted, dressed as they were in long sleeves and black habits. Hoping to be useful, we volunteered to play with the children for a while so the nuns could take a break. Then we realized that the girls didn't speak English. Twenty-five of them aged eight to twelve stared at me, and I stared back at them, not knowing what to do. Using hand gestures, I indicated that we would play a game.

The first game that came to mind was my old standby, duck, duck, goose. I got them in a circle and tried to figure out how to teach it to them when we did not speak a common language. First, I acted out what a duck was, waddling around and quacking as loud as I could. They finally understood the word "duck" and repeated it back to me. I didn't know how to convey "goose"; I had used up all my creativity with "duck." "Goose," I said, indicating an animal with a long neck. "Goose."

Thinking that I had made up the word, they burst into riotous laughter. I tapped Lisa as the goose, and she chased me around the circle. The girls, who were used to prim and proper nuns, had never seen two grown women do anything like this before. They thought it was absolutely hilarious. All of a sudden, it no longer mattered that Lisa and I were strangers who spoke a different language. We had broken the ice.

As luck would have it, the UNICEF translator arrived just then and the girls were able to teach us a game that involved play-acting. For a few brief moments, I didn't feel like I was in an earthquake zone. Playing with these girls, I could have been anywhere.

Of course, I wasn't just anywhere. Moving to an outdoor courtyard, I sat under a tree to interview a number of the girls about their personal experiences during the earthquake. I never had to do this before in an emergency situation, and I felt strange asking these children to revisit such a horrific memory, and one that was so fresh. We spoke to the girls one at a time as bleating goats meandered about, picking through the rubble, and as other girls played jump rope and talked.

"Where were you when the earthquake hit?" I asked my first interviewee.

Her tender smile disappeared, and she stared at the ground. "I was at school. The day of the earthquake, the bell rang about an hour before everything happened, so we were outside. That's why I wasn't hurt. My parents are okay, but they can't take care of me anymore. They don't have any way of getting food."

Apparently, this was a common situation: many of these children still had living parents, but with their houses and livelihoods destroyed, the parents couldn't provide for their children, and so these girls had become economic orphans. My heart went out to them as I thought of my own family history. My mother and uncle, upon arriving in the United States during the Holocaust, had relatives in New York City, yet these relatives were so poor that my mother had to live in an orphanage and take care of her younger brother herself.

Another girl, about ten years old, sat down next to me. "Let me tell you what it was like," she said solemnly. "I, too, was outside my school playing. Then the ground began to tumble and the school collapsed."

I leaned in a little closer to her. "Can you describe it to me?"

She gazed up at the heavens and her eyes lit up. "At first, I thought that G-d had finally taught me to fly, because my feet were no longer on the ground." She took my hand and looked me right in the eye. "But then I realized that my feet were where they were supposed to be but the earth wasn't where it was supposed to be."

"Well, what did you do?"

"We were very scared. Everyone was screaming and it felt like it was going on forever. Sister told us to pray. We locked our arms together and we prayed and prayed. I squeezed my eyes closed and asked G-d to help me."

I closed my eyes and imagined these young children locked in prayer as the earth shook. My heart just about broke, until she added, "And you know what? G-d heard me."

"How do you know that?" I asked, my voice cracking a little.

She smiled. "Well, because I'm still alive!"

"Of course," I said, hugging her. "And let's thank G-d for that."

As I continued to interview children, I heard a similar theme over and over, and it changed the way I saw Haiti. Innocent children—and the people of Haiti in general—were survivors because they willed themselves to be. From their viewpoint, G-d didn't choose to damn them with an earthquake. G-d chose to save their lives. Not only that: when

I asked what I should tell children in New York City, each girl at the orphanage told me that I should tell them to stay in school. "You don't realize how much you appreciate school until you can't go to school or it's gone," they said.

In Haiti, beyond ordinary faith, there is an extraordinary faith, the kind that emerges unpredictably and mysteriously in a time of need, so that sufferers can redeem themselves and carry on.

I wish I could say that deeper insight into the endurance of faith was the primary fruit of my time in Haiti, but that was not the case. As on previous trips, I also took back with me to New York a visceral sense of extreme human suffering. Over the next couple of days, we visited a school, and I taped personal messages in different locales to say thank you to the large organizations that had donated supplies or other resources to the relief effort. A few hours before I was scheduled to return to New York, I found a spot where the devastation was in plain view, put down my backpack, and walked to the top of a pile of rubble to tape such a message. Across the street about a half-block down, a man was sitting on a lawn chair, sobbing. He was far enough away that I couldn't hear him, but out of the corner of my eye I could see his body heaving.

We finished taping, and I looked down to pick up my purse. To my shock, I noticed the bony part of a human foot peeking out of the rubble. "Oh my G-d, it's a foot!" I screamed, stepping back. I recognized this object as a foot because my dad was a podiatrist, and we had kept lots of models of the bones in my house growing up. I fought back the nausea, realizing that for the last hour of taping I had been standing on top of a buried body, and G-d knows how many others that were down there. It was a horrible moment for me.

But it wasn't over. A man walking by had heard me scream. "Now you can understand why that man is crying," he said, pointing up the street. "His girlfriend had been in this building on which you're now standing. He has been sitting here every day waiting for them to remove her body. And he's going to continue sitting there until they do."

"Why haven't they taken it out yet?" I ask.

"They can't. They don't have the tools and trucks. They're digging with spoons and pails. It's going to take a long time. And that man intends to stay here for as long as it takes."

During my flight home, I was a wreck. Where in my brain and in my heart would I put what I had just lived through? You know how sometimes when you see a really powerful movie, the kind that transports you to a different time and place, you feel disoriented upon stepping out of the theater and back into your own life? Imagine that times a hundred. And this wasn't a movie—it was real and more terrifying than anything Hollywood could come up with.

Back in New York, I had an even harder time readjusting than I had had after Darfur or Sierra Leone. The devastation I had seen had been so tremendous that I was left wondering how long it would take for Haiti to recover when there was no solid government in place. It was easy to get depressed about it. On the other hand, I kept seeing that innocent ten-year-old girl at the orphanage saying, "G-d heard me. I'm alive!" And I had to believe that Haiti would endure. Haitians had a fire in their belly, strong enough that they would keep chipping away at the rubble with their spoons and pails, even if it took them years. They would rebuild. I just knew it.

Much to my chagrin, it seemed like so few of my fellow Americans shared that perspective. During the spring of 2010, the media had apparently grown impatient with the pace of change in Haiti, and they began to present a skewed and highly unfair picture of what was happening. To listen to nightly news broadcasts, you would think that nobody was doing anything right in Haiti, that aid money was being wasted, that corruption was rearing its ugly head again. If, in fact, a certain amount of this was happening, the real story—the great spirit of the Haitian people that I had seen firsthand, as well as the determination and benevolence of the aid workers—was going entirely unrepresented.

Imagine if you lost your school, prized possessions, parts of your home, your loved ones, and then someone asked you to clean up and rebuild with only a spoon and a pail. Although Haiti's progress was slow, it was substantial. When you consider that the United States, with all of our financial might, our strong system of governance, and our immediate access to tools, supplies, and support, still has not rebuilt entirely from Hurricane Katrina, you can begin to put Haiti into context. The media, however, evoked stereotypes of Haiti as a banana republic in some measure responsible for its own incapacity to handle a natural disaster. Americans were being dissuaded from giving aid, and those who had already given were beginning to regret their generosity. That was just wrong.

I wasn't about to sit there and see the good people of Haiti bashed. Nor would I stand by as Haitian children continued to suffer for lack of housing, clean water, adequate nutrition, medical care, and other necessities. There was an ongoing crisis here, and we in the developed world needed to step up. In an effort to convey the truth that I had witnessed first-hand, I talked to any audience I could about Haiti, trying to make people understand that Haitians were not lazy or un-deserving of aid. They were not just sitting back and asking the world for money. They were a proud people who were doing the best they could with the means at their disposal. And they deserved our support.

As part of this effort, I decided to visit Haiti again to gauge how much progress had been made. I wanted to take donors with me, so they could see what their dollars had done, and what future donations could continue to do. In October 2010, I led a group that included representatives from UPS, 1199 SEIU, and NBA star Dikembe Mutombo. When we arrived in Port-au-Prince, I found rubble strewn around everywhere, but the airport was repaired and now had air-conditioning, a luggage retrieval system, and even a steel drum band entertaining travelers. People begging for money still thronged us, but this time authorities were visible, and they stamped my passport. Rather than a no-man's-land, I felt like I was entering an actual country. That alone was some-thing to cheer about.

I realized, though, why people back home perceived a lack of progress. My travel companions hadn't seen the full picture of the initial devastation, so when they now walked off the plane, all they saw was how much rebuilding work still re-mained to be done. As we left the airport and drove around Port-au-Prince, they were aghast at how primitive conditions still were. "You have to understand," I told them as we passed an open area next to piles of rubble. "When I was here before, that open area was full of tents, because people had nowhere else to go. Now they have housing. That's progress. You have to compare it to what it was like before."

Our UNICEF Haiti colleagues filled us in on what had been happening, and there was quite a bit of good news. Almost two thousand of the four thousand schools that had been destroyed were already reopened. Tent cities such as I'd seen in the stadium still housed about a million inhabitants, but that was down from the estimated 1.5 million people initially displaced by the quake. As we drove around Port-au-Prince, we saw that the city was functioning again, with hotels, restaurants, and shops open for business. Checking into our hotel, we found that it had a pool and a bar, and that our rooms had working showers and sinks—a far cry from the tent I had to stay in before. Most of the city still hadn't been cleaned up, but there was a palpable sense of order and normality characteristic of civilized society. It was a poverty zone, but no longer a bleeding disaster zone.

Over the next few days, we toured many of the places that I had visited the first time around. Again and again, I saw positive changes. Even at the tent city, I found fewer residents, less squalor, and better access to water and medical care. "How can people live like this?" my fellow travelers kept wondering, while I kept thinking, *Wow, what a difference nine months makes!*

Nothing else demonstrated to me the progress Haiti had made in a relatively short time more than the reopened schools we visited. These facilities were generally semipermanent, open-air structures constructed of low-slung cinder-block walls, with poles extending out of the blocks to support a tin roof. They were walled in on one side, with a chalkboard hanging on the wall and tables with benches for the children to sit at. At one school for girls, we greeted several rows of polite, happy children wearing unbelievably crisp, clean, white shirts. These shirts surprised me; I knew that water was still at a premium and that some of these children were still living in tents or amidst rubble and dust. How did they keep their shirts so immaculate?

I didn't put the question to the class. Instead, I asked how many of them remembered the day of the quake.

All hands shot up.

"How many of you lost someone special in the quake?"

More than half the hands went up.

"How many of you are still living in tents?"

Again, half the hands went up.

"Would anyone like to tell their story?" the teacher asked.

One girl, about thirteen years old, stood up at her seat. Tears came to her eyes, and she broke down sobbing. "I and my friend were at my mother's house, and my mother was cooking dinner and needed something at the market. So we went there, and on the way home the earthquake happened. When it stopped, we went back home and the house had collapsed. My mother was dead."

All of us were crying now, too. I didn't want to end our meeting on this note, so when we had all recovered a bit, I asked the class if I could pose a silly question. "How do you keep your white shirts so clean?"

The girls broke into giggles. Raising their hands, they told me that most of them walked over an hour to school every day in the heat, wearing the one white shirt each had been given. When they returned home from school each day, whether to a building, a shack, or a temporary tent city, they each immediately got their buckets out and washed their shirts. They grabbed the edges of the shirts, pulling them "just so," to remove as many of the creases as possible. Then, when the shirts started to dry, they folded them around their notebooks, put them underneath their mattresses, and slept on them all night so that they would be ready for the next day.

"Really?" I asked. "You do all that?"

"Uh-huh," they responded, not thinking much of it.

In their eyes, school was invaluable; this was a far cry from how so many children in the United States seem to see it. My own kids wear ripped jeans to school; perhaps they can afford to do that, because they have been given so much. These girls have nothing, not even a permanent home to go to, but they do have their schooling as a source of pride, and they do everything in their power to hold on to that.

I returned home more determined than ever to stick up for Haiti and help raise money. If these little girls can walk in extreme heat, sit on uncomfortable benches to learn, and wash their shirts because they believe that getting an education is one of the most important things they can do to help their country rebuild, then who are we to dismiss Haiti as a lost cause? Who are we to deny the possibility that someday this country will take its place among productive, developed countries?

After this second trip, as I prepared my speeches and enjoyed time with my family, I found myself reflecting a great deal on the nature of perseverance. We all have our breaking points, and some people will give up sooner than others. Yet where precisely we break might surprise us. It doesn't compare with the complete devastation in Haiti, but when my dad died and I was eight months pregnant, people asked how I handled it. What else was I supposed to do? I couldn't change reality. I had no choice. Likewise, what choice did people in Haiti have? They could either give up or persevere. The majority had persevered.

We have this place deep down inside that is immeasurably strong. We have much more capacity to persevere than we think, and it was awesome to see that capacity at work with the people of Haiti. I used to regard heroes as people who had done unique, unimaginable things: saving a child's life or standing up to a bully. After visiting Haiti, I decided that sometimes my heroes were people whose whole lives had been destroyed but who day after day took a breath and resolved to carry on, have faith, and pursue their dreams anew. The girls in Haiti and their white shirts reminded me, as people in Darfur and Sierra Leone have, that the human spirit can be stronger than the strongest winds, the longest famine, the loudest rumble of the earth.

I didn't have to look very far to find heroes to look up to; my mother loomed even larger to me than she had before. At the age of seventy, she went back to school and fulfilled her dream of receiving a college degree. As I mentioned, she had arrived in New York City as a small child, not knowing the language, penniless, without her parents. Not long thereafter, she would discover that much of her extended family had been wiped out by the Nazis. For all this hardship, I had never heard her complain. In fact, during a conversation we had while preparing this book, she told me that she felt that she was "born under a lucky star." When I asked what she meant, she said: "One has to have the will to survive. My father had had the ability to pick himself up and go on—that's something he passed on to us. You take life in stride and make of it what you can. I have friends who are doom and gloom. I am fortunate not to have that outlook on life."

"Why don't you feel like a victim?" I asked.

"I don't know. Maybe it's because being strong allows me to look back at the Nazis and say, 'See? I survived!' We can choose to see ourselves as victims or we can choose to rise above what happens to us. Receiving the pity of others isn't a gift; it's diminishing. We have to look inside ourselves and do what we can to rebuild our lives."

As of this writing, Haiti continues to recover, although the earthquake's impact remains visible in the country's infrastructure, institutions, and social systems. All told, some sources report that the quake has affected about 3 million people, killing 316,000 and injuring roughly the same amount. To make matters worse, a cholera epidemic broke out in October 2010, leading to 7,000 additional deaths. Since it was the first time in living history that Haiti experienced an outbreak, people lacked the knowledge and capacity to prevent and treat the disease. Still, by the end of 2011, UNICEF reported that the number of displaced people had fallen to a little over half a million, including 220,000 children. Many of the country's longstanding problems, such as poverty, malnutrition, infant mortality, and wealth inequalities, are still in evidence, and probably will continue to be for some time.

UNICEF continues to make slow but steady progress reconstructing infrastructure and strengthening systems on the ground. By December 2011, the organization had reconstructed about 193 primary schools, provided hygienic facilities at an additional 198, improved and protected water systems for 1,430,000 people in rural areas, disseminated learning materials to 750,000 students, and opened 520 child-friendly spaces, among other accomplishments. As for my team and I, we wound up raising almost $70 million in support of these efforts—far more than I had ever expected.

As the Haiti earthquake fades from public awareness, I continue to think about the little girls with their white shirts and to feel the power of their presence. There was a time when I, like many, had been inclined to feel pity and see myself as a great savior swooping in. Now I know better. I sing it from the mountaintops, over and over again, as loud as I can: when you see people in the wake of a disaster, do not only count what has been taken from them; count what they have left. They may have been traumatized by the disaster, but they are not merely its victims. They are also its survivors.

6. RESPECTING TRADITION, BRINGING CHANGE

Peru, August 2010

It's one thing to feel that you are on the right path, but it's another to think that yours is the only path.

—PAULO COELHO, *THE ALCHEMIST*

"TRADITION. Without our traditions, our lives would be as shaky as . . . as a fiddler on the roof!" Thus proclaims the main character, Tevye the milkman, in the opening and closing scenes of the classic play *Fiddler on the Roof.* The theme is also present in the play's music and lyrics, which famously examine the relationship between traditional culture and modern progress, questioning how much of each is needed to achieve health and happiness, and begging audience members to consider when tradition might trump progress, and vice versa.

As a Jewish person growing up in the United States, I had not only seen *Fiddler* but had lived the conflict between tradition and modernity myself. Yet I never confronted this issue quite as powerfully as I did in 2010, during a UNICEF expedition I led to Peru.

Our first family trip to Brazil had been such a success that there was no question we would organize a second one the next year. By January, before we had selected a country to visit, I was already beginning to receive calls from parents wanting to reserve the very few spaces available. Overwhelmed with the demands of fundraising for Haiti, I turned planning responsibilities over to two members of my team and asked that they check in with me before making any final decisions. We already had a good model in place for making a trip like this, and I was confident my team would build on it.

Setting to work, my colleagues researched countries to visit, taking into account time zone changes, amenities on the ground, and UNICEF ground staff in each location (since the personality and knowledge of our host could make or break the trip). They concluded that Peru, like Brazil, would allow us to experience the realities of poverty without forcing us to rough it too much. A visit to Machu Picchu would give everyone on the trip an added bonus—a bit of vacation within a trip devoted to learning and working. On a personal level, I had always been captivated by Peru. Having received a book of South American folktales when I was five or six years old, I had conjured up all sorts of images about the country's historical wonders. My elderly aunt, who had given me the book, had visited Machu Picchu, and she described it to me as majestic and unbelievable. A visit to Peru was on my list of dreams at a very young age—and I had not yet managed to do it!

I was excited for other reasons, as well. After the intensity of Haiti and a completely hectic travel and appearance schedule, visiting Peru would allow me to step back and spend time with my younger son, James, who would accompany me. His schoolteacher had visited Peru the summer before and had shared photos of it with the class, so I knew just the idea of going there would alleviate any apprehension James might have had about joining a UNICEF field trip.

At age ten, James marched to the beat of his own drum and was busy defining who he wanted to be. Unlike other kids in his class, he grew his hair long, played the euphonium, and spent part of his summer learning amazing magic tricks. We had always judged him a wonderful kid with an extraordinary imagination. When he was only five or six, almost everything that came out of James's mouth was sung, leaving his dad and me in hysterics. Questions were not asked, statements were not orated—he just seemed to be living in an opera.

When James was six, he was diagnosed with a minor case of Tourette's syndrome. The effects of the disease ebbed and flowed, sometimes evident and painful, other times less so. On bad days, parts of his body twitched, especially his facial muscles, toes, and fingers. These involuntary movements would repeat as often as every twenty or thirty seconds. Because of my frequent travel, I had often worried I might not be there on a day he might need me to translate his disability to other kids, their families, or his teachers. Without a doubt, balancing the traditional role of motherhood with the modern role of the professional woman had called for constant calibration—something I hoped this trip would make just a little bit easier, as the Brazil trip had.

Fortunately, James had proven himself incredibly resilient. One afternoon shortly after he was diagnosed, I took him to the first day of a basketball program I had signed him up for. It was what I call a "heavy Tourette's day"; his face was forced into a bizarre grimace, his eyes rolling back. I had wanted to arrive at the gym before the program started so that I could tell the coach about his condition, but we got there late; the coaches were already addressing a group of about fifty children.

James sat down and paid attention. A few minutes later, the coach stopped talking and pointed at James. "Hey, kid, are you making faces at me?" My heart nearly broke. Ever since James started having symptoms, I dreaded a moment like this when he might be called out in public for being different. But James didn't miss a beat. "No, coach," he said. "I'm not making faces. My face just does that, but don't worry, it doesn't bother me." That's James—just an amazing, sweet, good-humored kid whose ability to observe and laugh at himself has been some compensation for what he has had to endure.

Intellectually, a visit to Peru interested me because it would allow me to sharpen my thinking about global inequality as well as UNICEF's approach to addressing it. Over the past few decades, differences between rich and poor countries were narrowing, but economic disparities within countries were getting worse. In many countries, the problem was not simply pervasive poverty; certain social, racial, and ethnic groups suffered disproportionately from extreme poverty— and attendant health and welfare problems—relative to the rest of the population.

In 2010, UNICEF's executive director, Anthony Lake, had published a paper introducing UNICEF's Equity Approach, arguing that we could best reduce child mortality and improve maternal health on a global basis not by simply pouring aid into a country and dispensing it to the population at large, but by serving the poorest of the poor first, even if they were harder to reach geographically. As the paper stated, "Reaching the most deprived and vulnerable children has always been UNICEF's central mission. But recently it has become an even more pivotal focus of our work, as emerging data and analysis increasingly confirm that deprivation of children's rights are disproportionately concentrated among the poorest and most marginalized populations within countries."[1]

Peru is an ideal place to see the equity approach in action. The country's approximately 30 million people are ethnically diverse: roughly 45 percent are indigenous American; 37 percent are mixed indigenous and European; 15 percent are European; and the rest are black, Japanese, Chinese, and other ethnicities. Some areas of the country are remote, including regions in the Amazon River Basin and the Andes mountain range. Peru has seen rapid economic development and significant declines in poverty and rural poverty.[2] Yet living conditions, access to services, and the vulnerability of children vary between indigenous and nonindigenous children. An estimated 78 percent of indigenous children come from poor households, as opposed to 40 percent of nonindigenous children; 45 percent of indigenous children live in extreme poverty.

Even within indigenous populations, equity issues loom large. Children whose first language is a native Amazon language are the poorest and most disadvantaged of all; 86 percent of these children come from poor households, and 49 percent live in extreme poverty. Children from Amazon tribal groups suffer from higher levels of mortality, malnutrition, and anemia, and they enjoy less access to safe water and sanitation, education, and timely birth registration.

Although a number of factors have contributed to these trends, a lack of inclusive government policies stands near the top of the list. Because of policies that favor dominant groups, many local communities lack culturally pertinent public services as well as the relevant, quality information they need to plan and deliver these services. Indigenous populations often don't participate in defining policies and adapting them to their cultures, nor do they receive equal access to public monies and other resources.[3]

In line with the equity agenda, UNICEF's operations in Peru had protected excluded children and their families by promoting the universalization of rights and the eradication of inequities. The UNICEF Peru team advocated on behalf of indigenous children with national policymakers, implementing programs that addressed issues such as neonatal mortality in rural areas. To truly improve something like neonatal mortality, we needed to put in place technologies and training for the critical care of newborn babies. But we couldn't just throw in new technology and practices; we needed to align them with community beliefs, traditions, and practices. Tevye's singing ran through my head as I read about this challenge and how we might address it.

Before the visit to Peru, I believed my past experiences in other countries, as well as my earlier work on civil rights and diversity issues, had taught me what I needed to know about respecting social and cultural differences. I would discover, however, that while I had grasped the concepts, I had not yet appreciated just how profoundly cultural differences affected the work of helping individual children and families—how time-honored cultural traditions could prove the difference, for instance, between reducing child mortality and keeping rates stagnant.

Visiting Peru, I would learn that an approach that helps the poorest first really does work best. And I would see that the poorest of the poor aren't simply passive recipients of aid. Rather, they have important perspectives about how to better their lives on their own. Like the women in Darfur building their child-care center out of bricks they made by hand, Peruvian villagers I would meet would confirm how crucial it was to work alongside those receiving aid, helping local communities find unique solutions that bridged traditions and modern medicine. Paulo Coelho had it right: there is not one right path, but many, and we go astray, despite our best intentions, when we arrogantly assume the contrary.

James and I arrived in the Peruvian capital of Lima early on a Tuesday morning, traveling with some members of our group from New York. We had the day to recover, do some sightseeing, practice our Spanish, and introduce members of the group to one another. Despite the relaxing vacation elements of this trip, I was still a bit anxious. Our family field visit to the Amazon had been a special experience in large part, I thought, because I had handpicked members of the group, so I had known that everyone would get along. This time, we had invited a number of outstanding donors and supporters, but I did not know all these individuals equally well. Also, while the first trip had been only mothers, this time we had a father with us, changing the group dynamics. I doubted we'd be spending as much time together talking about menopause as we had last time. But what would we talk about? If everyone didn't get along, it could potentially be a very long week.

Altitude was also a concern. Although Lima was at sea level, we would be traveling in the Andes at elevations as high as thirteen thousand feet. That's over two miles into the sky—a height that would test most novice skydivers. I had heard stories of tourists who had had serious trouble breathing while visiting the Andes, no matter what kind of physical condition they were in. During a briefing call before the trip, I asked the other parents if they were worried about altitude sickness, and they said no. I asked our country director in Peru, who had decided to bring his two boys along, if he was concerned. "I've taken the guys around," he told me, "and they've always been fine." Weighing all the pros and cons of going to Peru, I felt secure that we had made the right choice, but there was no way I could know for sure.

With its 8 million inhabitants, Lima is a busy urban center, lined on one side by tall, glassy apartment buildings that run along the Pacific Ocean. Despite its seaside location and fog, the city was surprisingly dry, clocking in as the world's second largest desert city, behind only Cairo, Egypt. As our group trickled in, we decided to take a leisurely tour of the historic downtown center, a UNESCO World Heritage site. On the van ride over, I watched our kids interact with each other, asking questions about school, sports, and music. Two pairs of travelers would join us that evening, so our group was just small enough to easily navigate the tourist attractions.

Our group reacted with oohs and aahs as we entered the town square lined with pastel-colored, Spanish colonial–style government buildings and a beautiful baroque church. Some of us believed we spoke enough Spanish to communicate effectively, and we decided to test these beliefs by volunteering to buy entrance tickets and translate signs we were seeing. (Some of us passed the test; others, not so much.) As we toured a particularly old church, the kids wanted to explore a catacomb and ventured in together, squealing with excitement at the skeletons and tombs. I couldn't have been happier that they were bonding.

The adults were fantastic, too; along with two members

of my immediate staff, we were joined by a member of our Gala Committee; a young mother of three from Westchester, New York, who runs a wonderful girls' mentorship program; and a board member from Long Island who is a physician and mother of five. In the evening, we would be joined by the chair of our board in Chicago and his daughter, and a businesswoman from Boston who was new to UNICEF and her son. Our Peru country director, an American, would bring his two sons, who split their time between Lima and their home in Brooklyn, New York.

At our welcome dinner that evening, we dined on local ingredients—quinoa, potatoes, ceviche—at a restaurant situated at the base of an amazing ancient ruin right in the middle of Lima. Lit from the base with strings of bright bulbs, the whole structure seemed to shine a magical green, the light refracting against the clay. While we ate, we talked about Lima's size, reviewed some basics about the trip, and discussed Peru's UNICEF programs. To help make the trip more enjoyable, I took careful note of everyone's questions, hoping my staff and I could help them find the answers as the trip progressed.

The following day, we woke at dawn to meet our final group members at the airport and take an hour-long flight to the ancient city of Cuzco, elevation eleven thousand feet. Flying over the Andes to Cuzco is similar to crossing the Rocky Mountains on a transcontinental voyage across the United States. Snowcapped mountains dominate the view, with green hills and small farms dipping down into shallow valleys. During our approach into Cuzco's dusty airport, we saw giant figures arranged on the hillsides surrounding the city, as well as an Incan ruin on a large hill.

As we taxied in, I noted a clear uptick in the group's

anxiety about the altitude. Would we feel it? What do you do if you can't breathe? As if on cue, we stepped off the plane to find airport vendors selling blue and green cans of oxygen, a flash of color against the white, stuccoed airport walls. Many of us playfully took pictures. "How funny, oxygen at the airport," someone said. "Maybe I should bring one back as a souvenir." Meeting one of our UNICEF staff members from the Cuzco office, we boarded a small bus. "How are you feeling?" we asked each other as we hauled our luggage. "Do you need help carrying anything?" My suitcase had not seemed that heavy to me in Lima, but now I was dragging it beside me, my lungs burning. I couldn't tell if I was experiencing some type of psychosomatic reaction to the altitude because we'd been talking about it so much, but it felt real enough.

We traveled an hour or two out of the city on winding roads to the inn where we were staying. It was a harrowing drive. This area of Peru, the Sacred Valley, is a familiar tourist destination, popular around the globe. But the roads are narrow, there are no guardrails in many places, and the buses travel at uncomfortably high speeds. I tried to distract myself by taking in the view. The mountains were spectacular, taller than any I'd seen. Although we had descended somewhat from the elevation in Cuzco (part of our plan to allow everyone to adapt to the high elevations), we were still at some eight thousand feet above sea level.

Pulling into a long dirt road, we saw a rustic building up ahead. The inn, built simply of rough-hewn wood, was situated directly on a whitewater river at the foot of a mountain. As we got closer, we saw that the inn consisted of a number of separate buildings with terra-cotta roofs. The main building, built to conform to the shape of the mountain behind it, stood two floors high and consisted of a row of rooms connected by an outdoor wooden walkway. The walkway also joined up with the lobby building, which held a few couches and a pot of coca tea (a drink thought to aid adjustment to the altitude). Checking in, I was delighted to find that each of our rooms had a private porch. It was so wonderful gazing over the railing at a narrow, rocky stream and breathing exceptionally fresh air into my lungs.

After some downtime to unpack, we reconvened as a group in a small field behind the inn. The temperature had dropped, and we had all switched into long sleeves. Dinner that evening was an exercise in avoidance—that is, avoiding the small insects that overtook the hotel's dining room. There were far too many to count, and we found ourselves taking refuge under white linen napkins found at each of our places. The carefully prepared and beautifully arranged food arrived, and we attempted to eat while also doing our best to avoid the bugs. It was not pleasant, but it was also such a strange and unexpected situation that we soon found ourselves laughing.

As we exited the dining room, we were greeted by an orange and pink sunset so breathtaking that we all stopped to take it in. We were still looking up at the sky when a group of ten to fifteen Peruvian elementary schoolchildren arrived to spend time with us. We greeted them in Spanish, but many spoke only the native Peruvian language, Quechua. To help break the ice, we formed a circle and threw a ball of string from person to person. Each person who caught the ball had to say his or her name, identify something he or she enjoyed, and then throw the ball of string to someone else, becoming symbolically connected to that person via the string. Soon everyone was laughing and throwing the yarn at increasingly challenging angles; the whole group was connected by something that looked like a spider web. With our local UNICEF colleagues translating, our children discovered that even though they didn't speak the same language as the Peruvian children, they had similar tastes in music, food, and sports. Huge grins broke out on all their faces.

Guided by our local UNICEF team, the Peruvian kids had planned an evening program for us that began with a traditional song and dance performance, followed by a session in which they attempted to teach the songs and dances to us. A few members of our group caught on easily, but most of us found ourselves tripping over our feet and mispronouncing the lyrics—a performance that elicited good-natured laughs from the Peruvian side.

Next, the Peruvian children told us that they wanted to show us the "river of rights" that they had created as part of a UNICEF program. As it was now very dark, they led us to a covered, lighted porch where they unrolled a long piece of paper—about twelve feet long by two feet wide. On the paper, the class had drawn a river in blue with twists and turns along the way as well as rocks jutting out. These rocks each represented various "rights" that children have in life—the right to education, the right to be protected from violence, the right to health, the right to be included. The UNICEF team translated each word, leaving us all impressed by how clearly our organization was helping to educate and empower these indigenous children, a vital step toward positive change in their community.

Our kids clapped, but the Peruvian children weren't finished. They wanted to talk to our kids, hear their perspective. What were children's rights like in the United States? What protections were our children fighting for? The questions brought puzzled looks from our kids. Although they went to some of the best schools in the United States, they'd never thought at length about their own rights as children. They took for granted that they were guaranteed an education, and that a legal framework existed to protect them from adults who might do them harm. It hadn't occurred to them that having a birth certificate was a right, or that it was their right in the United States to have access to a hospital.

I encouraged our children to talk about some of the freedoms they had as U.S. citizens. "We have freedom of religion," James said. The translator explained this to the Peruvian children, and they nodded. Another said, "Freedom of speech—we can say what we want!" More nods. Pretty soon the group was telling stories and having a conversation about rights. I felt sorry that we hadn't prepared our children for this discussion in advance but happy that the discussion happened organically. It was our first serious interaction with children in Peru, and it was leaving a mark.

We ended the evening with a big bonfire, accompanied by singing in Quechua and English. Wearing black-and-white costumes made of tissue paper, the Peruvian children performed a "crow dance," flapping the wings of their costumes and acting out a traditional folk tale in time to the music. Before we said good-bye, we all lay on our backs on the lawn, gazing at the expansive night sky, much as our previous group of intrepid travelers had done while floating down the Amazon.

Early the next morning, I awoke and looked over to find James's bed empty. It took a few minutes to break through the early morning fuzziness and get my bearings. Where was I? What country was I in? Panicking, I got up to go look for my son. I checked the bathroom, but he wasn't there. I was about to call down to reception when I saw that the door to the back porch of our room was open.

I peeked out and was relieved to find him sitting in a chair and looking out into the countryside. "Mom, isn't this magnificent? It's just breathtaking." I had to agree that it was. Three separate lines of mountains came together right in front of us; they were brown and rocky and teeming with goats. In the immediate vicinity of the hotel lay gardens with large purple flowers; next to them, the river, bright blue in the early morning light; next to that, tall evergreen trees. The colors were majestic, and James couldn't take his eyes off of it. He had been there for an hour already, watching the sun come up.

The only thing more special than this landscape, I thought, was the fact that James had noticed it. Living in hectic New York City, I so wanted my children to be able to stop and smell the roses. How amazing to know that James was sensitive enough to appreciate natural beauty, and that he had sought it out all by himself, enjoying a private moment, without feeling the need to wake me or another child in our group. In my travels, no matter where I went, I, too, found myself gazing at my surroundings all the time, appreciating their splendor and thinking, *Gosh, I'd really like to paint that scene someday.* Often upon returning home I had been unable to describe what I had seen. This trip was different; James had seen beauty, too, and we would share the memory of it forever.

Later that day, our group traveled to the nearby town of San Salvador to speak with the mayor and learn about the condition of children there. San Salvador was a medium-sized municipality whose small, modest buildings were built along the same river that cut through the entire Sacred Valley. I wasn't sure if our kids would have the patience to sit through an official government briefing, but I was pleasantly surprised, no small thanks to the mayor. Not only was he ruggedly handsome—bronze-colored skin, brown eyes, a full head of thick black hair—but charming and quite a charismatic speaker.

The mayor welcomed us into a small room, dividing the adults and children into two groups. The kids moved into another room, while we adults engaged in a lively discussion about the Sacred Valley's child-friendly municipalities, towns like San Salvador that have agreed to focus on protecting and promoting children's rights. The mayor challenged us to consider what might make a city worthy of being called "child-friendly." He told us that people in his town had recently realized that if they were to meet the needs of children, they needed to engage children in helping to create the solutions they were seeking. Thanks to the support of UNICEF, all of San Salvador's children had been registered and had birth certificates; chronic malnutrition—a critical concern for Peru—had been reduced considerably, and the access of children to preschool education with an intercultural bilingual focus had improved by 74 percent.

Next door, our children were learning about "participative budgets"—a subject that sounds bureaucratic and boring but is actually quite interesting. In San Salvador, the local government was investing money better on behalf of children by allowing local children and adolescents to help determine how the money was spent. I'd heard about this type of programming in Brazil as part of their UNICEF Seal of Approval programs, and here was a different twist on a similar model.

Interacting with elected government representatives, organized groups of children and adolescents engaged in discussions with government leaders, taking a seat at the table where decisions are made. They had raised a range of ideas—from training to recreation programs, school supplies to health education. In many ways, the process mirrored student governments one saw in the United States; adults of these communities were demonstrating to children that they were important, and they were putting their money where their mouth was. In 2009, the child-friendly municipalities gave priority to projects that took into account the proposals of children (mostly in connection with improving the quality of education). I wondered: How would my children choose to prioritize projects in my town of Bayside, New York? Had they ever considered it?

After our meeting with the mayor, we took a short walk down the dusty, narrow dirt roads of San Salvador to a local school. I was very excited about this portion of the trip: The UNICEF office had arranged for our group to paint a mural on the walls of an elementary school with the children there. Back in college, when I was studying studio art, I truly felt that the act of creating something new and expressive broke down all boundaries, and now I would experience that first-hand. The kids at this school were adorable, wearing bright uniforms that contrasted sharply with their dark features and hair. When we were first introduced, they circled around us, singing songs and speaking Spanish with us.

We accompanied the children into a small, clean classroom, where we all sat down to color and play games. Teachers handed out a snack bag for each child filled with quinoa cookies. Finally, we made our way outside to paint a mural on the school's wall, covering it with fun scenes portraying everything from a playground to large letters and numbers. I grabbed a paintbrush and joined in, working on a scene already in progress that depicted a group of kids playing. I had noticed that one of the kids in the picture was wearing a bright blue shirt. Picking up the can of white paint, I carefully placed the word "UNICEF" on the shirt. "There," I thought. "Now people will know what brought us here."

Observing our group, I took note of how wonderfully James was doing. Here he was, in a foreign country with a group of children he didn't know, yet as we painted the murals, he was talking to everybody and was happily engaged with the activity. Looks like he was turning out to be a pretty good warrior, just like me. Yet his ability to adapt would soon be put to a considerable test, serving as both a reminder of how different life is around the globe and an object lesson on the limits of cultural exchange.

On the third day of our trip, we were scheduled to visit a child welfare surveillance center in an isolated town called Chumpe, some 12,500 feet above sea level. I had tried to research Chumpe before we left the United States, but I couldn't find much online. I did learn that the climate was cool and often damp and foggy due to the altitude, and that the people here lived much the way their ancestors had— simply, close to nature, and in extreme poverty. Lacking other options, most people in Chumpe made their living as peasant farmers, surviving the rough climate by steadfastly adhering to the concept of *ayni,* basically translated as, "Today I help you, tomorrow you help me." They also relied on traditional spirituality, their worship of the Pachamama (Mother Earth) and the Apukuna (mountain and nature spirits) more recently infused with Christianity, particularly Catholicism. I was anxious to see this village and observe to what extent their reliance on ancient culture and tradition was sustaining them.

We rode from our inn in the valley up into the mountains on a bumpy, winding dirt road. I gripped my stomach as we wove higher and higher, again swerving at high speed around terrifying curves with no guardrails, as on a roller coaster. Gazing out the window, I noticed that the vegetation was becoming sparser, and that the relatively modern houses and shops had been replaced by cruder structures of mud brick and thatch. Locals at the higher elevations seemed to wear more traditional clothing, the women dressed in lively pinks, oranges, and blues, their hats appearing to me like colorful and ornate napkins edged with trim. And ponchos—even the men wore them so as to protect themselves from the cold temperatures.

Upon boarding the bus, I had noticed a large, metal oxygen tank in one of the seats and thought to myself, "Uh-oh." Sure enough, it became harder to breathe as we continued up the mountain. Near the top, the road became too steep for our bus, so we had to get out and take jeeps the rest of the way up, hiking on foot into the village. We found the temperature much cooler and villagers wearing knitted winter hats, heavy capes, and shawls, all patterned in extremely bright pinks, yellows, and reds.

When we arrived, we received a warm welcome from parents, children, health-care workers, and other representatives of the Chumpe community. They took us around the village and proudly informed us about their efforts to promote children's early growth and development and their success in improving maternal health care and reducing malnutrition.

We visited an early-childhood center where local NGOs, supported by UNICEF, were administering programs that kept track of children, starting from when a mother first became pregnant. Entering two small square rooms constructed with cold concrete and little insulation, we met a group of young children led by a young woman working for the NGO. The children sat down on rugs and played with one another quietly, kneeling over from time to time to grab one of the toys that one of the staff members had set on the ground nearby. These toys—wooden blocks, a small plastic drum, stuffed puppets—helped the children develop their motor skills.

I remember thinking how tiny these children were, yet how well-behaved. Poster boards lined the walls of the small clinic, filled with specific information related to individual families and children in the area. Maps—all hand-drawn in colorful ink—depicted where every pregnant woman in the area lived. Graphs drawn in green and red ink reported the number of cases of malnutrition in children under three years old between 2001 and 2009; during that time, the percentage of Chumpe's children receiving adequate nutrition rose from just 38.9 percent to 80 percent. Another chart listed two women, ages twenty and thirty-one, who were currently pregnant in Chumpe, along with a list of important checkups that the center would facilitate throughout their pregnancies. Each time one of the woman was treated or cared for, the center would mark an X on the poster. This was a maternal health to-do list in action—and one that had drastically reduced the numbers of mothers dying in childbirth.

Around lunchtime, we played soccer with the local schoolchildren, presenting them with soccer balls as a gift. All the kids were so excited that they took off running, kicking, and showing off their best moves. The game began, and everyone seemed to be having a great time. Then I looked over and was shocked to find that James had turned green. "My head hurts, Mom," he said, coming over to me. "Real bad."

I pulled him aside. "Okay, stop playing. Let's have you sit down in the jeep until you feel better."

Sitting in the jeep didn't help him feel any better; he was gasping for air. "Does anyone have an oxygen tank?" I asked. We had only one other tank, and another child in our group, the son of the director of our Peruvian team, was already using it. "Do you mind if we use that for a little while?" I asked the boy, but he refused us, shaking his head.

I faced a dilemma. This other boy wasn't having nearly as much trouble breathing as James was. The mother in me wanted to rip the tank out of his hands and give it to James, but the staff person in me had to approach the situation delicately and try to convince the other kid to give up the tank voluntarily. I tried some niceties and then got a little more direct. "Look, you've been sitting here for ten minutes with the air canister. James isn't feeling well; he needs air. Don't you think you could share?"

He finally agreed, and we put the mask around James's mouth. James took two breaths and then pulled the mask away from his mouth. "This isn't working, Mom," he said, gasping. I inspected the canister and found it was empty. Now what? James was looking more and more fatigued and unsteady; I thought he would pass out. I needed to get him off that mountain. But that would cut the visit short for others in our group, who were still enjoying the game and the chance to interact with the villagers.

Seeing my distress, one mother in our group came over to

offer her help. "I could take James off the mountain while you finish here. It would be no problem."

I considered my options. "It's a kind offer," I told her, "but I'm going to take James down myself. He's my child, and I'm a mother before anything else. Could you please let the rest of the group know what's going on? I'll meet you at the bottom when our session is over."

James and I strapped on our seat belts, and a member of our Peruvian team drove us in the jeep down the mountain to another village at the bottom where they had a UNICEF-supported health clinic. Two other children in our group weren't feeling so hot, either, so I brought them as well. I watched the scenery go by, trying to distract myself from thinking about what conditions at the clinic might be like.

In Mozambique, I had toured rural clinics and been shocked to find primitive huts or semipermanent structures, records kept on paper rather than computers, simple wooden benches for the patients to sit on. I'd since come to appreciate how vital local health clinics were in developing countries, how accurate their records really were, and how attentively the care was given. Still, this was my first time experiencing health care as a patient (or at least, as the mother of a patient) in a developing country, and I admit that I was nervous. It's one thing to observe progress in developing world medicine from a bystander's point of view, quite another when your own kid's wellbeing is at stake and you're panicking.

We arrived at the clinic, and I was relieved to find it equipped with electricity and running water—more modern than I'd imagined. Still, the conditions here were a far cry from what we were used to in the States. The floors were grimy, and the uniform the receptionist wore was old and stained. The center lacked adequate ventilation, and probably a budget for janitorial services and cleaning supplies, so it smelled of urine, sweat, and disease. *Okay,* I thought to myself. *I can't afford to be diplomatic right now. If James needs serious care, I'm out of here. I'll have him airlifted to Lima.*

Thinking of his experiences in New York hospitals and seeing no desk by the front door, James asked: "Where do we sign in?"

"We don't," I responded. "They don't do that here."

The receptionist led us into an examination room and we met the doctor, a lovely woman wearing a clean white coat. I felt grateful that there was a doctor here; as I'd seen in Mozambique, most rural clinics in developing African countries were staffed with less educated health-care workers. But now another problem arose: the doctor spoke no English. Normally this wouldn't faze me, but with James looking sicker by the minute, I didn't want to rely on a translator to describe what was wrong with him to the doctor. Glancing at James, I sensed that he was equally unsure. The doctor listened to his heart, looked at his eyes, and took his blood pressure. She rattled something off and my colleague translated. "She does not think there's anything seriously wrong with him. She suggests we give him some oxygen and see if he feels better. If not, we can talk about other options."

James looked at the oxygen equipment, and I could see he was worried about the amount of dirt on the tank and mask. He seemed to weigh it out in his mind: risk the dirt and get oxygen from the tank, or don't risk it and quite possibly remain ill. To my relief, he grabbed the tank and inhaled. The doctor left to attend to other business. After about fifteen minutes, James felt much better, and color began to seep back into his face. The doctor popped her head in again, asking a question in Spanish. My colleague translated: "Now that he's feeling better, would you like us to show you around a little?"

I agreed that this would be a good idea. The doctor arranged for a nurse who spoke English to take us around. Our first stop was a basic lab. "This is the centrifuge we use for running blood tests," the nurse pointed out proudly. James asked how it worked, and using hand motions, sounds, and half-translated sentences, the doctor explained the process. The lab was actually pretty well stocked. It was not very large, but there appeared to be a variety of test tubes, thermometers, and other supplies available.

We continued on our way, stepping over strewn papers and other items left in a hallway, and then turned a corner into another long corridor. Out the window, I saw an attached building that appeared to house a series of tiny rooms, each closed off with a curtain. "Ah," the nurse said, responding to my query. "Women in labor stay in those rooms until they are ready to deliver. This way they are not too far away when the time for the actual birth arrives."

We now entered a room that had the distinct smell of blood in it. "And here," the doctor said in Spanish, "is our birthing room. We're very proud that so many women from the area come in here to give birth rather than doing it on their own at home." Indeed they did come; a patient had apparently given birth that day, and I was appalled to find the floor still spattered with blood and scattered with papers. In the United States, this mess would have been cleaned up right away, but not here. James was starting to look green again, although this time it was not from lack of oxygen, but from the sight and metallic smell of blood.

"What's this?" I asked, pointing to what looked like a padded chair back with no seat bottom.

"It's where women give birth," the nurse said.

"You don't use a table or a bed?"

"No, no. Many local Peruvian women prefer to give birth squatting. They don't believe lying down is healthy. When we first opened this clinic, we had only tables. But women were not coming to use the clinic; they preferred to give birth at home as their mothers had done. We knew we would have to find ways to make this clinic more acceptable to them. We began by asking people in the community about their traditional birthing methods, inviting them to tell us what was wrong with our clinic. We learned so much! First, they complained that the doctors did not speak the local language, Quechua."

I understood that. I had just experienced how difficult it was to have confidence in a doctor who did not speak my language.

The nurse explained that the women pointed out that the clinic did not allow husbands and other family members into the delivery room, while at home a woman gave birth surrounded by loved ones. And they hated the hospital gowns they were asked to wear at the clinic. Finally, the table. They absolutely refused to give birth lying on a table. Squatting was more comfortable.

The doctor nodded her head. "Although Western medicine has long preferred lying down, others believe the most natural position for giving birth is the upright position. We had a decision to make: was it better to adapt our clinic to be more in line with the local traditions and thereby get women to use it more, or should we hold to our ideals and have the local women continue to give birth at home and without medical attention?"

Their answer was obvious. The birthing stations were installed, and other changes were made.

My mind was racing. As in Mozambique, I was struck by the great diversity of experiences and cultural norms that exist around the world when it comes to childbirth. When I had given birth to James and Lee, I had never even thought about doing it at home; I had simply assumed that the way to give birth was in a hospital, under medical supervision. But we weren't finished yet. As the doctor told us, women who had come here to give birth stayed for a day or two to rest up. We walked past the rooms designated for this use, and I noticed there weren't any nurses here waiting on them, bringing them breakfast in bed. These women were expected to care for themselves. Those who had other young children had brought them with them, lacking other childcare options. One woman pulled back the curtain to her room, allowing me to see inside. There was a small cotlike bed and a chair. Tucked under the bed was a cooking pot the woman had brought with her, and lying in the middle of the bed was her recently born son. Nothing else.

Knowing the rest of our group would soon be coming down the mountain, we concluded our tour. The doctor took one more look at James and assured me he had just been suffering from altitude sickness. Through the nurse, she stressed that I should pay close attention to his sensitivity for the rest of the trip. I did keep James especially close, although it was clear he was fine. We spent the next days sightseeing at Machu Picchu and another spectacular site, an old Incan fortress called Sacsayhuamán. Here again the intersection of modernity and tradition came to the fore, with our guide remarking: "In this area of Peru, the Inca culture is apparent. People live in balance with the land. They may be more modern today, but as you look around Machu Picchu, you can see that the Incas were way ahead of themselves." We looked at the water system and structures they had built and could only wonder how they had done so. With that idea fresh in our minds, our time in Peru came to a close. We said good-bye to the Sacred Valley, flew back to Lima, and took a second, longer flight home.

In the days that followed our return, James and I had a chance to talk about the birth clinic, and I reflected that I had gotten a more visceral understanding of what social disparities really mean. In an article called "White Privilege: Unpacking the Invisible Knapsack," Peggy McIntosh recounts that men never thought they had a special place in society until women's studies came along and pointed it out. Likewise, whites in our society are not taught to recognize the privileged position they enjoy because of their race. I now realized that being born in an industrialized country produced an analogous effect. I still took so much for granted, even after all the experiences of other societies that I had had. I was surprised at the raw emotions I'd felt when it was *my* kid whose health was on the line.

I was impressed at the way the clinic had adapted itself to meet the needs of the local women. Birthing rituals may seem like minor details, but they go to the heart of what organizations like UNICEF do in communities around the globe every day, determining whether local residents avail themselves of our services or not. Since UNICEF lives within the communities it serves, it has long understood that success demands a joining of modern science with local norms and traditions. Many parts of our Peru trip bore out how valuable this approach is: the participative budgets that gave local children a voice, the decision to offer bilingual education (in Spanish and Quechua) in the schools, the school curricula that incorporated local tales and legends. I was left wondering, though, where the line was. Are there limits to how much we should respect local cultures if doing so means that more babies and women might die in childbirth? Is there a point beyond which Western medical knowledge should win out?

Before joining UNICEF, I had dedicated eighteen years of my life to teaching antibias skills, getting people to respect other cultures and cultural experiences. Yet sometimes local traditions are so unsafe that their potential harm outweighs cultural sensitivity. This is the case with female genital mutilation or with tribal traditions that claim that AIDS could be cured through sex with a virgin. In these cases, aid organizations have no choice but to adhere to what science knows to be best. But in other cases, a difficult balance needs to be struck. In Peru, I had seen firsthand the power of acknowledging that local people can indeed have the right answers—the right answers for *them*.

My Peruvian trip calls to mind other encounters I have had that evoked the power of local differences and experiences. In my first month on the job, one of my UNICEF colleagues who grew up in a small, isolated village in Nepal shared a personal story with me. He had an opportunity to go to Columbia University, and his family saved every dime to send him. To stay in touch, he wrote letters, and it took three weeks for the letters to reach the village and for him to receive a response. Soon after arriving in New York, he wrote to his grandfather about life in the United States, describing the tall buildings and the first elevator ride he had ever taken. He explained his apartment, describing each piece of furniture—a sofa, a kitchen table—with the knowledge that no equivalents existed in his village. Even silverware needed explanation, for at home he had never used such utensils.

My colleague went to great lengths to explain the forks, spoons, and knives Americans used. Three weeks later, a response from his grandfather arrived. "I liked what you told me about your new world. I was particularly taken by the description of the place you are living in. But I was concerned with one thing. I must tell you that if you're dining with people with knives at the table, then you're dining with the wrong people!" In his grandfather's village, knives were only used as weapons. It was inconceivable that they would be used in a friendly way as eating utensils.

All of us see the world through the filter of our life experiences, education, and customs. I don't have an easy formula for balancing science and tradition, but I do know that we must recognize the power of tradition, as the character Tevye reminded us at the beginning of the chapter, and we must also understand and respect what others value. When I was doing diversity management work, we often challenged participants to consider changing the golden rule from "Do unto others as you would want done unto you" to "Do unto others as *they* would want you to do unto them." We need to become more adept at asking questions, listening to answers, and integrating that learning into solutions.

Even in cases where modern science is too compelling to ignore, development work makes most headway not by simply imposing modern science on local cultures but by showing deference to the culture and giving local communities the tools and information they need to decide to change it. A great example of a group that does this is Tostan, which has had incredible success in Senegal convincing thousands of people living in local villages to abandon female circumcision. Rather than simply imposing Western practices, telling villagers that their traditional practice was bad, the organization educated local community members about the practice and its practical implications (including increased infertility) as well as what science had found, engaging in an extended dialogue that spread outward from workers to schools to the local village to surrounding villages. In an interview, Tostan's founder, Molly Melching, a woman I greatly admire, explained the theory Tostan has deployed as well as why it has worked.

"Humanitarian workers in the West have a tendency not to take local cultures seriously," says Melching. "But in fact, they're incredibly powerful. When you have a traditional practice, behavior or cultural, something people have always believed is good, and someone from the outside tells you to stop doing that—well, that probably is the worst thing you could do, even with the best of intentions. It has no meaning for the local people who are doing what they're doing because they believe their practice is not merely good, but a religious or spiritual imperative that will affect the fate of their souls. That's powerful stuff. So you need to educate people, and in their own language. Until adults who have never been to school have information that allows them to dialogue with people in their community, you can't make headway. That takes an incredible amount of effort. But it's worth it."

Tostan taught villagers about the development of the

child, the brain, every organ and body system, explaining which practices favored good development and which hurt development. Where Tostan's workers realized that strong social norms were coming up against medical science, they allowed for lengthy discussions and information gathering, asking local community members to think about the gap between what they wanted for their community and what traditional practices were actually doing. Eventually, with all the facts in hand, villagers came to the conclusion themselves that female circumcision was destructive, not merely to women but to the social and economic wellbeing of the community as a whole. Change proceeded from there.

Tostan realized that the decision to abandon traditional practices for Western ones had to be organic, coming from the inside out. And for some deeply rooted practices that conflicted with Western medicine, such as female mutilation, change would only come with public declarations on the part of local communities that they were formally deciding to embrace change. "Even the most deeply entrenched local cultures can change," Melching related to me, "but the local communities have to want to commit to it. They have to draw the line in the sand themselves. They have to say, 'As of tomorrow, we won't be doing such-and-such any longer, and those who do will be sanctioned by society.' It's sort of like those Christmas parties you go to and everyone has brought gifts even though everyone secretly doesn't want to be giving and accepting gifts. The practice will only change if everyone together joins hands and proclaims once and for all that the rules are going to change and we will all behave differently."

I continue today to ponder the balance we must strike between respecting traditional cultures and changing them in beneficial ways. And I continue to admire development efforts like Melching's that respect local cultures and engage with them on the deepest level, even if it takes more time and effort.

In my personal life, I have found that I have become more culturally sensitive because of my experiences in the Andes mountains. While I have always believed in celebrating differences, and while I have dedicated much of my career to preaching that, I have not always invested the time needed to understand the value of those differences. I initially assumed that women who covered their faces for cultural reasons were repressed and secretly wished to uncover them. Yet in many conversations I have had with these women since visiting Peru, I have come to learn that they feel empowered by only sharing their faces with their husbands. Several have even remarked that they feel *more* sexy, not less, when they are covered up. Who knew?

Tostan means "breakthrough," as in the hatching of an egg. The word also means spreading and sharing. If we are to continue to make progress remedying inequalities, we will need to become more sophisticated in working with differences, acknowledging and bridging them, creating hybrid cultural realities that synthesize old and new. We must spread and share with open hearts, mindful not merely of our own rightness, but of the complex web of traditions that make every cultural group unique and worth knowing. In helping others, let's stop trying to make them like us. Rather, let's empower them to break through their own challenges themselves, in their own ways, taking time as well to reexamine our modern truths bestowed by modern science. Make no mistake—without science, the world's children will live shorter, more troubled lives. But without tradition, they also risk teetering and falling, becoming every bit as vulnerable as fiddlers on a roof.

7. THE BAG MAKERS OF BANGLADESH

Bangladesh, February 2011

Childhood should be carefree, playing in the sun; not living a nightmare in the darkness of the soul.

—DAVE PELZER, *A CHILD CALLED "IT"*

AT FIRST GLANCE, Dhaka, Bangladesh, is an unruly city—throngs of people, smog, crumbling buildings, traffic that barely moves. Dhaka is the most densely populated urban area in the world, over 15 million souls living in an area the size of Portland, Oregon. But it is also a city of flowers and politeness and warmth, of spicy food and phenomenal breads. Like Peru, it contains a mix of old and new: cars driving alongside rickshaws and pushcarts; dilapidated houses next to sparkling retail malls; locals in modern dress conversing with friends wearing traditional garb.

When I visited Dhaka in the late winter of 2011, we began our day in the slums. Residences here were stacked right next to one another, lining both sides of three- to four-foot-wide alleyways, their overhanging aluminum roofs blocking the sun. We found ourselves bounding around piles of garbage, stagnant water, and live chickens. The stench was unbelievable. And everywhere we looked, there were children of school age who were not in school.

I had done my homework and was aware that over 7 million children in Bangladesh between the ages of five and seventeen were working.[1] Given the grinding poverty of their families, they had no choice but to put in long days as carpenters, boat builders, fabricators of shopping bags, and domestics in people's houses. The least fortunate worked as prostitutes, selling their bodies to eke out a meager existence. In the interviews I had read, the children repeatedly spoke of this situation as their inescapable fate. They had no hope, saw no other future for themselves. This was their life, and it would continue to be their life.

My travels had so far overturned many of my preconceptions, yet I thought I at least understood a basic truth about children and adults: they were fundamentally different. Adults were expected to be mature; kids were not. Adults were accountable for their actions, their words, their deeds; kids were forgiven their errors. Adults were expected to take life seriously; children were afforded their right to be silly. Above all, I always regarded childhood as a special time for dreaming, wonder, and play. On my desk, I keep a quote from Robert F. Kennedy that reminds me to hold on to that piece of childhood still within me: "I dream things that never were, and I say, 'Why not.'"

I came away from this trip with an important and enduring piece of wisdom: being grown up isn't defined by your age. Children around the world are forced to shoulder responsibilities and burdens that many would find appalling and extreme. And adults everywhere can often behave in selfish, unfeeling, or immature ways—like children.

As of 2008, an estimated 215 million boys and girls under

eighteen performed labor, over half in unsafe workplaces.[2] Boys tended to work in more dangerous jobs on farms and in factories, where the risk of injury was great, while girls worked more often in domestic settings, where they were often mistreated or abused. Both situations rendered these children unable to dedicate themselves to school. Although roughly 90 percent of the world's primary-school-age children are enrolled in school, only 60 percent of secondary-school-age children are. In some regions, the statistics are worse. For example, the percentage of secondary-school-age children who attend school dips as low as 36 percent in sub-Saharan Africa. Significant disparities exist within countries and across genders.[3]

The issues around child labor are complex and vexing; taking into account economic and cultural realities, I cannot claim to know exactly where the line between childhood and adulthood should fall. Many families depend on the wages of the children to survive, which means that they often can't go to school. But if they don't go to school, how can a family ever break the cycle of poverty?

On another level, child labor isn't so complex. Childhood is all too often a luxury when it should be a basic right available to all. Those of us fortunate enough to live in nations that protect this right need to ensure that all children receive this protection. It is not enough to save a child's life; that child must be able to grow, develop, learn, and have a chance to succeed. Children must enjoy childhood as fully as possible—dreaming, playing happily in the sun—and it is up to us, the adults of this world, to step up, take responsibility, and make that happen.

I first learned about Bangladesh during my own childhood, thanks to popular music. In 1971, acting on a request made by his good friend and fellow musician Ravi Shankar, George Harrison organized the famous Concert for Bangladesh, turning the country's name into a household word. Intended to benefit refugees displaced by war and natural disaster in Bangladesh, the event took place at Madison Square Garden before more than forty thousand people, bringing together the day's leading musical artists, including Eric Clapton, Ringo Starr, Bob Dylan, Billy Preston, and Badfinger. It was the first concert of its kind, using music as a catalyst to get people on their feet and help those in need.

The Concert for Bangladesh and its related products not only succeeded in raising millions of dollars in humanitarian assistance for UNICEF over the years, it brought global awareness to an entire generation of young Americans. I remember watching a famous press conference between George and Ravi in which reporters asked them why, with all the problems in the world, George saw fit to focus on Bangladesh. George's answer was so genuine it has stayed with me. He looked at the reporter and with characteristic humility said, "Because I was asked by a friend if I would help, you know, that's all."

An album of the concert was released, and everyone I knew spent hours listening to it on their home stereo, blasting the music in support of Bangladesh. I was fourteen years old when it all happened. The war in Vietnam was raging and we relished being part of something that brought Americans together to save people in a place few had heard of— simply because they were human beings. In my wildest dreams I could not have imagined that all these years later I would not only visit Bangladesh, but do so in the company of Olivia Harrison, George's widow, a woman I have come to call my friend and whom I admire greatly.

I first met Olivia at her home in Los Angeles in 2007, shortly after I became CEO. George had died in 2001, and the U.S. Fund for UNICEF had been working with Olivia since 2003, collaborating on how best to use dollars from a fund Olivia had set up after her husband's death, the George Harrison Fund for UNICEF. I have to admit that I was extremely nervous about meeting her, as George had been one of my teenage idols; I even had a poster of him on my bedroom wall. It was surreal walking up to the front door of her home in California, ringing the doorbell, and wondering if George Harrison himself had crossed this very threshold.

Moments after we were introduced, all my nervousness dissipated. I found Olivia to be intelligent, soft-spoken, incredibly kind, and a wonderful host. Jonathan Clyde of Apple Records, who works on the Fund with her, was also present. He was humorous and warm, and both were so unassuming that they put me at ease. I shared my vision for connecting youth in the United States with children around the world, and we brainstormed about how we might integrate George's legacy into that vision.

I will admit, it was hard to stay focused. Family pictures of George and Olivia, along with their son Dhani, adorned the house, catching my eye as I glanced around. I was listening intently to what Olivia and Jonathan had to say, but also remembering teenage days spent singing Beatles songs like "All You Need Is Love" and "Hard Day's Night." I tried to describe to Olivia and Jonathan the impact George's music had had on my life as well as how clearly I remembered his statement describing his link to Bangladesh.

Over the next couple of years, Olivia, Jonathan, and I continued to build the George Harrison Fund for UNICEF, integrating it into our grassroots work on college campuses.

The fund helped increase our campus groups' fundraising by matching all monies raised each year, in addition to making significant grants to UNICEF programs in Bangladesh and other places around the world. In 2010, realizing that the fortieth anniversary of the Concert for Bangladesh was coming up, we looked for a way to celebrate the occasion while also advancing George's legacy of giving. It was a big year; Olivia was working with Martin Scorsese on a documentary about George's life that promised to generate major publicity, and we decided to honor the whole Harrison family at our annual Snowflake Ball in New York, recognizing them for their four decades of dedication to children through UNICEF. We knew the time was right to make this "the year of George."

We decided upon a trip. Despite decades of involvement with Bangladesh, Olivia had never been to the country, and neither had George during his lifetime. Our immediate objective was to visit a number of programs that the George Harrison Fund for UNICEF had invested in on behalf of the children of Bangladesh. It would be an emotional trip for Olivia, coming around the tenth anniversary of her husband's death and given her own longstanding friendship with Ravi Shankar. The government of Bangladesh wanted to honor George Harrison and the family, and it promised to be a once-in-a-lifetime experience for all. I relished the chance to be a part of it, even as I girded myself for another heartbreaking encounter with children living in extreme poverty.

Landing in Dhaka's airport, I joined my chief of staff, Brian Meyers, and Olivia, Jonathan, and a few others. Olivia was weary after hours of traveling, but she gave me a big hug. "I can't believe I'm actually here." Observing the tears in her eyes, I realized just how personal an experience this was for her. She was here to perpetuate the legacy not merely of George the musician but of George her husband.

We drove through the streets of Dhaka, and I was shocked at how unbelievably crowded they were. Pedestrians, bicyclists, and motor vehicles were all moving in different directions but somehow finding their way, hemmed in by lines of four- or five-story buildings. Legions of rickshaws flowed past, weaving in and out of traffic. We passed shabby, derelict buildings as well as lean-tos, the latter seeming to serve as private dwellings or shops. Bangladesh was cohosting the World Cup of Cricket with Pakistan, and we observed English-language advertisements for apparel and business development placed on crumbling buildings—a strange juxtaposition indeed. At open-air markets, hordes of people sat on milk cartons buying and selling. Beggars in rags approached our car at red lights, holding out their hands. The sheer press of people was overwhelming, as was the pollution, primarily diesel fumes. Even in the car, we placed rags over our faces so that we could breathe. I remember Olivia passing around Fisherman's Friend cough drops, which helped erase the taste of pollution in our mouths.

When we finally arrived at the UNICEF office, we entered through gates guarded by armed Bangladeshi soldiers. Their green fatigues and red berets were not exotic to me, as I'd encountered Bangladeshi UN peacekeepers all over the world in places like Haiti and the Sudan. I found the UN building in Dhaka, a large concrete structure, aging but functional. Key members of the UNICEF team greeted us, all eager to meet the group, and especially Olivia.

In Bangladesh, George Harrison is viewed as a hero of the

nation's struggle for independence. Every year on Independence Day, the Concert for Bangladesh is played on the radio. We knew how much interest and attention Olivia's arrival in Dhaka would spark, so we had purposely kept details of our trip private to minimize possible disruptions and allow her to make the most of her visit.

We began with our usual briefing, delivered by members of our Bangladesh country team. Located in Southeast Asia and bordered by India and Burma, Bangladesh was founded in 1971 after declaring its independence from Pakistan. Undeveloped and extremely poor at first, the country had made great strides in reducing poverty and infant and maternal mortality, registering children at birth, and providing access to clean water. Still, much remained to be done. Almost half the Bangladeshi population of 156 million lived below the poverty line, with per capita earnings of about $848 a year; almost a third of the country lived on less than $1 a day. Almost half of children under five were stunted, and only about a third of women and just over a half of men in the country could read. Education remained a challenge, with fewer than half of all students completing primary school and attending secondary school. Culturally, parents had little or no understanding of how play and other informal learning could prepare children for school. And perhaps most startling of all, the most common cause of death for children under five years old was drowning—owing, we learned, to the terrible floods the country suffered each year during monsoon season.

UNICEF had been helping in a number of ways. Programs in place supported childhood immunization, maternal health, good nutrition, HIV prevention, and better access to safe drinking water. UNICEF's Early Learning for Development project provided centers for child care and education to the most vulnerable children between the ages of four and six. Most of these kids were living on the street, but social workers supported by UNICEF located them and brought them to the centers. Because many families relied on income earned by their children to survive, another project for working children focused on nonformal education that fit in around children's regular work schedules. The project established small learning centers in urban areas; children between the ages of ten and fourteen attended morning classes for two and a half hours, six days a week, and returned to their place of employment after class. To combat high rates of child marriage, UNICEF was also running an adolescent empowerment project, sponsoring adolescent centers where trained leaders educated their peers about children's rights, child marriage, reproductive health, gender, dowry, and violence. Drop-in centers served some five thousand street children, giving them basic education as well as food and shelter.

We began our formal program by again navigating Dhaka's bustling streets and visiting a center for preschool children located in a quieter area. We were mobbed by people as we exited our trucks, but I never felt concerned for my safety. While the sheer number of people was sometimes overwhelming, the people themselves were always smiling and often even walked arm-in-arm.

We entered a small, warm classroom decorated with posters and children's art and a colorful red, blue, and yellow floor mat. I chuckled as I saw a poster in the back of U.S. President Barack Obama arm-in-arm with Muhammed Yunus, Bangladesh's most famous citizen and founder of the successful Grameen Bank, which provides microloans to families across the country. The children here were adorable, the girls dressed in ornate traditional saris and dresses, the boys in Western clothing. They were thrilled to see us, laughing, giggling, smiling, holding our hands. We sat in a circle and played the requisite game of head and shoulders, knees and toes. Olivia and Jonathan sat on the floor with the children and composed drawings with them on portable chalkboards. The opportunity for play and discovery in this center was amazing. It truly was a pioneering place in Bangladesh, where the idea of preschool is virtually nonexistent. These kids were getting a head start in life, and it was wonderful to see.

From there, we made our way across the city to Balur Basti, Bangladesh's largest slum. The agenda said we were visiting a basic education center for working kids, but it was difficult to conceive of anything like that existing in this place. Located along the banks of the river and separated from the city by a road, the slum consisted of narrow dirt alleyways wending between attached bamboo shacks where whole families lived in single rooms. We stepped over trash and raw sewage, trying not to choke on the stench that seemed to permeate everything. Young children mobbed us, singing and holding hands, very excited by our visit. Punctuating the alley's darkness were brightly colored rugs and clothes that residents had hung out to dry on the walls. Peeking down an alley as we walked by, I saw a family of five squatting in a circle, with what looked like an eight-month-old child sitting in a diaper on the ground. I just couldn't imagine trying to raise a family in these conditions.

We continued on our way, passing a well-like structure made of brick, with flies buzzing around and fetid water running at the bottom; we learned that this served as a water supply for slum residents. After walking through more narrow alleys, we passed into a clearing where garbage littered the ground in clumps and children walked about barefoot. Finally, we arrived at the center, little more than a walled-in space that UNICEF had "rented" in the slum and cleared of garbage. The smell was still there, but even so, this place was something of an oasis. A group of twelve to fifteen children sat around the edges of the room, all with blue UNICEF backpacks and art supplies. A large red oriental rug covered the center of the room, and children's artwork and writing were pinned to the walls, leaving the impression of a classroom you might find in the United States overlaid with darkness and the smell of the slum.

The children here were young—eight, nine, and ten years old—and they introduced themselves by telling us their name and "profession." Some were rubbish collectors, some worked as domestic help in wealthier people's homes, some labored in shops making garments or sorting fabrics. Any conceivable job that involved menial labor, you name it, and one of these children did it. Upon hearing these introductions, I physically flinched, so uncomfortable was I with the notion of any child this small working like an adult. I tried to picture my own children at the age of nine working as servants, or what it might be like to have a child cleaning in my own home, but I couldn't do it.

I also couldn't help but contrast the situation these children knew with what I had experienced growing up. Sure, I had worked since the age of thirteen, but strictly as a form of enrichment, a supplement to school. My first job was quite fun, putting up window displays and waiting on customers in a household goods store. I was treated as an adult, allowed to drink coffee with everyone else, and given my paycheck at the end of each Saturday. Afterward, I worked in a fast-food restaurant, then as an assistant in a doctor's office and as a secretary at our synagogue. On weekends, I babysat. All of my earnings were what my dad called "party money"— money to be spent on things for myself, when and if I desired them.

I went to college when I was only sixteen, and it was a disaster. I wound up dropping out and taking a few classes at a community college for a year and a half while living at home. I would go to class and then come home to a mother who was cooking dinner and doing my laundry. I was fragile, and I needed the time to sort things out, learn about who I was and what I wanted, negotiate the line between child and adult. These children in Bangladesh didn't get the luxury of time. They shouldered great responsibilities at age eight or nine, working instead of going to school, playing sports, or enjoying social time with their friends. My mother used to tell me, "It's okay, you're only sixteen; you don't have to have all the answers." These kids *did* have to have the answers—at a much younger age.

After finishing our time at the center, we briefly visited a home in the slum. It was a rickety, jerry-built structure on stilts, built to protect against flooding. Because of the stilts, getting up to the living area meant navigating a rudimentary ladder about eight feet high to a wooden walkway without protective railings. It was so treacherous that one member of our group slipped on the ladder on his way up. A small, naked child stood at the top of the ladder, and I couldn't help but cringe at the thought of her having to deal every day with these dangers. Inside the home, we didn't find much. The family sat on a mat on the bamboo floor; clothing hung from the walls, and blankets were piled around for sleeping— all of this in one room.

As we continued slowly out of the slum, a nine-year-old

girl served as our guide. Walking arm-in-arm with a friend, she led us along a trail of garbage and flies past a rudimentary, informal store that sold rice and other goods. On the fringes of the slum, we were introduced to a little boy who worked as a carpenter; he proudly showed us his workplace, a makeshift structure in an open space. The conditions were far from safe or clean. Young boys squatted in the dust amidst wood scraps and shavings, sanding and hammering as a foreman looked on. Nearby worked men using electric drills, saws, and sanders. They proudly displayed beautiful furniture they had built and just finished staining. None of the workers wore shoes, although nails and sharp objects were everywhere. We watched as the young boy slammed a hammer into a sharp tool used to separate two pieces of wood. My nine-year-old would never have been allowed near these tools, but this boy used them every day. Also, this boy didn't have goggles or other safety gear that is mandatory in the United States and other industrialized countries.

Next, we left the slum and drove a short distance to an outdoor marketplace, where the little girl who guided us worked. She was tiny, dressed in a bright orange traditional dress, with dark eyes and dark, shoulder-length hair; from behind, you would have said she was only six or seven. She was likely malnourished and stunted—more than half the children in Bangladesh are—and her clothes were faded and worn, yet they also possessed a certain beauty.

Although we had arrived at an outdoor market on a busy street, I soon realized that her vocation was not selling vegetables or goods. She led me into a long white building that housed shops on the first floor, but that clearly also held something underneath. The building appeared constructed of clay, and as we walked through a tunnel that led to the subbasement, all light disappeared, and I felt the air cool by a few degrees. The dark was claustrophobic; I felt as if it were closing in on me. In reality, the tunnel was not long, but the darkness was so thick that it felt endless. There was no point of reference; you didn't know where the walls were, yet all around you heard people moving, talking, and grunting. The tunnel also seemed to have collected all the unpleasant smells associated with extreme poverty. We had some security with us, but I was scared. We could disappear down here and nobody would ever know. I could not imagine how this little girl walked this way every day, usually alone, seven days a week, on her way to work. The idea of it terrified me.

Halfway through the tunnel, we turned left and saw a dim light shining through an opening. We entered a small, barren room with white walls and a cement floor lit by a single, uncovered bulb. It was an informal workshop that produced shopping bags out of plastic netting. The bags were small— the kind you might see holding clementine oranges around the holidays. A man sat at a table, cutting squares and dropping them onto the concrete floor. These squares were then picked up one by one by three young, skinny, barefoot girls who worked kneeling on the bare cement floor. For hours each day, they frantically stitched corners of the bags together one after the other, with no breaks, not even for food. Although these girls received only pennies for a full day's work, they considered themselves lucky, knowing that the alternative could be prostitution, begging, or worse.

Nearby on the floor sat a woman and two children. They weren't working; instead, they were playing and eating oranges. I thought this strange, so I inquired through an interpreter. I was shocked to learn that this was the workshop owner's family. They were passing the day in leisure, supported by the labors of children who, because of their poverty, had no current alternatives and a very dim future to look forward to. My UNICEF colleagues explained that they were working with the shopkeeper to improve the conditions and introduce basic standards, including meals, for these young employees. The only saving grace for the girl who had brought us to the store was that she had spent the morning at school. UNICEF offered subsidies for families who sent their children to school to help offset the lost wages. It was a small step, but it meant the world to these families, and it held out hope that they might one day break the cycle of poverty.

Later in the trip, Olivia and I would go out to buy saris. The shop wasn't especially colorful—a mall store like any you'd find in the United States. But the fabrics were sensational, laced with metallic threads, the colors bright and exotic. I couldn't enjoy them, because every time I picked up a piece of fabric, these little girls stitching shopping bags flashed before my eyes. Had a child made this piece of fabric, or was it made by a grown-up? And if it was made by a child, was purchasing it helping them or hurting them? I didn't want to encourage the practice of child labor; I wanted these children to be in school! But I also didn't want these children to starve, which is what would happen if they didn't have this source of income. I wound up purchasing a sari, but I went to bed that night turning all this over in my head, tormented by questions for which I had no answers.

That afternoon, while I was still struggling to process what I had seen in the slum, we traveled to the outskirts of the city, to the river delta areas of Dhaka that experience frequent flooding. Bangladesh is sometimes referred to as the land of rivers; the river Ganges enters Bangladesh from the north, taking on the name Padma once it does. Padma joins the Brahmaputra River (whose main flow is called Jamuna) in the country's center. Every year, the rivers enrich the region's soil, but they bring even greater destruction when they flood. Even knowing this, I was struck by the area's tropical beauty—lush green grassy plains and groves of palm trees spreading on the banks of the wide, flat river.

We got on to one of Bangladesh's few open roadways and drove in a convoy. After about an hour, we turned onto a small dirt road that ran along the top of a dikelike structure surrounded on both sides by rice paddies and small factories that make bricks. The combination of jet lag and the humming of the jeep's engine were making me sleepy. I was just closing my eyes when I heard someone cry out: "Whoa, watch out!"

The jeep lurched to a stop, jerking me forward and waking me up. I poked my head out of the car to see what had happened. I couldn't help but laugh. There, in the road, stood a large elephant blocking our path. A teenage boy sat on the elephant's back, smiling from ear to ear and in absolutely no hurry to clear the animal out of our way. He was enjoying every moment of the power he had to stop traffic. Teenagers are the same everywhere!

With some encouragement from our driver, the elephant passed and we continued on our way, arriving at the site of a school that teaches the art of traditional Bangladeshi boatbuilding. Yves Marre, the school's founder, first saw Bangladesh's waterways from a plane but was intrigued enough to explore the area. He was familiar with Bangladesh's long tradition of naval carpentry; for centuries, Bangladesh's waters had seen handmade wooden boats with large earthen-colored sails. Today diesel-powered steel vessels have replaced many of these magnificent wooden boats, and the art of boatbuilding is fading away. Yves and his wife, Runa, have taken it upon themselves to preserve techniques and knowledge previously passed on informally by generations of boat-builders in the region. At the school, master craftsmen are building replicas of the wooden ships that once floated on these rivers, assisted by student apprentices. As Yves proudly told us, high-quality vessels constructed by students had gone on display around the world. We toured the school, and it became clear that it offered a good, healthy environment for kids—a place where they could learn and grow, not merely be used for menial labor.

One of the men working in a senior position there, himself originally from Great Britain, showed us his home, a house that reminded me of the movie *Father Goose*. It wasn't a huge house, but it was built entirely of bamboo and fabric, its rooms divided by screens. When you sat on the porch, you could watch the sun set on the river. Just being here, I could understand why a person could happen on this spot and this house and never leave.

At the invitation of Yves and his wife, we got into a long, wooden, covered boat for a ride up the river. As we began to drift, they encouraged us to crawl onto the peaked, slanting roof to experience the view. There was no ladder, so climbing up meant grabbing on and pulling yourself up to sit on the roof. I took a deep breath, told myself not to look down, and after two tries, managed to shimmy up.

It was well worth the trouble. The riverbanks were lined

with long grasses, and as we floated by, we passed numerous oxen bathing in the river not far from where people were swimming. Small "country boats" floated past us, powered by small sails or oars. Occasionally we could see a village in the distance, helping us to understand just how remote they were. Yves explained his vision for transforming boats into movable schools that would allow children in remote, flooded areas to be educated. We could potentially build one large boat to house the school and use a fleet of many smaller boats to transport students from their homes.

Olivia was enamored with the idea as well as everything else we were seeing: the beauty along the river, the energy of Yves, and the skills of the kids who were going through his boatbuilding program. It was a pleasant journey—quite a contrast to the dank, windowless space where little girls were making bags all day. Our group was able to relax, let go for a little while, and enjoy the sail.

The next day brought us back to reality. We visited a center for at-risk youth in Mirpur, at the northeast end of Dhaka. Close to fifty children between the ages of five and fifteen gathered there each day. About thirty, some as young as four years old, lived in the center. All the kids were on their own, not supported by any family members, and all had once been street children. They are the offspring of Bangladesh's poorest, forced to live on the margins of society, neglected and deprived of basic necessities. The exact number of street children in Bangladesh is unknown, as no birth registry exists to allow for such a count, but it is estimated at over four hundred thousand.

These children are far from invisible. As we saw firsthand,

they approach cars stopped at Dhaka traffic lights, selling flowers or other goods. Many are abused or forced into prostitution. The lucky ones find their way to a center such as the one we were visiting, where they receive food, education, health services, and life-skills training. We were immediately struck by the opportunity these children had just to be children. At the center, they could play games and explore crafts and other creative outlets. Such pursuits seem trivial, but they are a critical part of children's development. In an article I had read about artwork created by street children, one of the girls interviewed had commented that she drew butterflies because she wanted to be like them, "colorful and happy." All children should have the opportunity to be colorful and happy.

We entered the center and were greeted with a performance on child rights. A moderator asked the children what their rights were, and they responded: "We have a right to shelter, food, education, health, and play!" They explored these rights in a series of skits and ended by singing a rendition of "We Shall Overcome." We were all overcome with emotion at hearing this song, which served as a key anthem for the American civil rights movement. In my youth, this song expressed strength, hope, unity, and perseverance. Apparently here at the center, it was doing the same thing. These young people were uniting and letting us know that they would prevail. It might take some time, but I have every confidence that they will.

I left Bangladesh with a fundamental question: At what age is a child a child, not an adult? Where and by what criteria does society draw the line? Where should *I* as a parent draw the line?

I had always assumed that human beings before the stage of puberty were children, not adults, and that society should treat them that way. In the United States, you have to be sixteen to learn to drive, eighteen to vote, twenty-one to buy and consume alcohol, and at least fourteen before you can work part-time. In my Jewish faith, thirteen is the age at which boys and girls are formally initiated into the community as full adult members. Yet in Bangladesh, the eight- and nine-year-olds I had met in many ways were adults. They were responsible for tackling grown-up decisions on the job, and they faced adult pressures to show up for work on time, day after day, and perform. They bore the adult pressure of knowing that the welfare of their families depended on them.

At the same time, these children remained children in just as many ways. When not at work, they yearned to play. They used the arts to push the limits of their world, dreaming of becoming butterflies, happy and colorful. They kicked soccer balls and giggled at soap bubbles when I produced them. When I asked where they hoped to find themselves someday, many responded by proclaiming their intention to become doctors, nurses, teachers, or policemen. They enjoyed games and playtime just as much as children their age in the United States did.

Some decisions I make about when and how to treat my own children as adults conform to socially accepted rites of passage, while others happen independently, based on my own judgments of their maturity: how old my children needed to be before I let them take public transportation alone, how late they could stay out, how far from home they could be, when they were old enough to date. Each of these decisions represents a step in the ladder toward adulthood, the point when I will let go and allow my children to make their own decisions. Hopefully, I will have prepared them well and given them the foundation on which to make strong adult decisions for themselves.

But what of the children in Bangladesh? Where will their foundation come from? And if society demands that they perform as adults at the ages of eight, nine, or ten, does that mean they have the right or ability to make adult decisions themselves and be left to their own protection? In developing countries like Bangladesh, where parents don't have the luxury to make choices, are we not *all* responsible for helping to guide them along the way? If I would not allow my own child to walk alone in a dark tunnel on his way to a basement workplace, how can I justify sitting back as another child does it?

Intellectually I know that Bangladesh's children must work, and that we cannot deny them access to much-needed income. But I cannot accept that fact without a struggle. I don't know precisely when children become adults, but I do know that a ten-year-old, even one forced to provide income for his or her family, cannot be treated as an adult all the time. We have a responsibility to ensure that as many children as possible are not robbed of their childhood—of a time to imagine, dream, play, become educated.

Working is by no means the only way that children around the world today are seeing their childhoods cut short. In developing countries, not including China, almost 25 percent of adolescent girls aged fifteen to nineteen are married, one out of three in South Asia.[4] Children are also forced to serve military functions. As UNICEF reports on its website, "Around the world, thousands of boys and girls are recruited into government armed forces and rebel groups to serve as combatants, cooks, porters, messengers or in other roles. Girls are also recruited for sexual purposes or forced marriage. Many have been recruited by force, though some may have joined as a result of economic, social or security pressures."[5] Child prostitution and sexual exploitation is another widespread social problem in many developing countries, including Bangladesh.[6] In all these cases, adults of the world need to step in and allow children to enjoy their precious childhoods as much as possible.

The average citizen in an industrialized country can't even begin to imagine what it's like to be denied a chance to dream. I know I didn't. Since visiting Bangladesh, however, I have been to so many centers for street children—in Kenya, Tanzania, and in other countries. I meet children who are adults in so many ways, but who come to these centers to play basketball—because they are still kids. The girls in these centers hold my hand and ask me, "Am I pretty?" Yes, I want to tell them, you are pretty, you are wonderful, and you are a child. You deserve so much better than the lot you have been dealt. And one day soon, your life may improve.

In Kenya, I once met a tribal chief who wore a gorgeous beaded headdress with three feathers sticking out. I told him how much I liked it. (He then tried to buy me for four goats, which I'm told is a good price, but that's another story.) This chief told me that he had made the headdress himself. I must have seemed surprised, because he looked into my eyes and said, by way of explanation, "I may not have much. As a matter of fact, I may not have anything. But G-d gave me hands. And G-d gave me eyes. And together, I can make beautiful things with them. That's how I made this headdress."

His words apply here. G-d gave us all hands and eyes, but maybe because we have so much, we fail to realize the beauty we can make with them. This man has nothing, but he dreams. And we need to give kids time to dream, too.

8. THE WOMAN IN THE DESERT

Kenya, Fall 2011

IN KENYA, at the height of the fall 2011 food shortage, I had an experience that has haunted me ever since. The trip started out easily enough. I first accompanied several of our donors to Copenhagen to meet the Duke and Duchess of Cambridge, more commonly known as HRH Prince William and his new bride, Catherine (Kate). Having gotten engaged in a remote cabin in Kenya, the royal couple had wanted to draw attention to the famine in Somalia and the food crisis in Ethiopia and Kenya, and they had turned to UNICEF. It was agreed that they would come to the global UNICEF supply center in Copenhagen, where they would be joined by Crown Princess Mary and Crown Prince Frederik of Denmark, to help pack two planes—a 747 donated by British Airways and a UPS-donated cargo plane—with supplies for children of the region. I and a few others would then accompany those boxes to Nairobi. From there, they would be delivered to those in need. We would get to deliver supplies ourselves to the children in the Turkana region of Kenya.

I had never met the royal couple and was excited. I had no

idea what the social protocols were. Would I have to curtsy? (No, not as an American.) How should I address them? (His and Her Royal Highness.) Was physical contact okay? (Handshakes only.) What should I wear? (Business attire.) Do I host them or allow them to walk freely through the room? (I host them.)

The U.S. Fund's vice chairman at the time, Peter Lamm, would accompany me on this trip. Peter is one of those guys whose tough exterior can seem somewhat off-putting when you first meet him. He comes across as all business, always concerned with the return on investment and efficiency. Get to know him, and you find he is bright, warm, a phenomenal friend, and a passionate advocate for children. I don't think there is another board member with whom I have argued more, but at the same time, I adore him. We're about the same age and height, making it easier to go head-to-head with one another. He has his own sense of style, rarely getting out of blue jeans and usually wearing cowboy boots. I dare say that although he's tougher than I am, we're equally pigheaded when we believe we are right. This was not our first trip together, and I was looking forward to sharing the experience.

Copenhagen is a beautiful old European city, although the cold and damp while we were there seemed to penetrate everything. We landed and headed straight to the supply center. I had never been to this facility before, and Peter, I, and a team from *ABC News* were able to take a tour before the four royals arrived. We were in awe. The building was enormous, covering 215,278 square feet, the equivalent of three soccer fields. It felt cavernous and stark, cement floors and walls offset by brightly colored artwork hanging on the walls and a steel ceiling almost two stories above. If not for the amount of activity going on, I would have thought I was strolling around a very modern—and seemingly endless—art gallery.

Learning about the activity here was as fascinating as any art gallery. UNICEF supply division executives leading our tour told us the facility could store thirty-six thousand pallets, representing over seven hundred and fifty different UNICEF supply items, such as scales, pharmaceuticals, therapeutic foods, and tents. The operation used the latest computer and automation technology to organize supplies and pack them into pallets. Forklifts rolled by, lifting the pallets onto a machine that wrapped them together in plastic. The pallets were then loaded onto a roller-coaster-like train that carried them off to be loaded automatically onto trucks, which in turn took them on the first leg of their journey to children in need. Peter and I remarked that neither of us had considered what a complicated task it was to get a particular item into the hands of a small child somewhere in the world.

But it wasn't simply individual items that were shipped from here; UNICEF created and sent sophisticated kits designed to fill specific needs. The Emergency Health Kit, something I had seen in the aftermath of the Haiti earthquake and used with other natural disasters, contained enough medicine, supplies, and basic medical equipment to help ten thousand people for three months. The surgical obstetric kit, which I had seen in Mozambique, contained surgical instruments, basic sterilization equipment, and resuscitation equipment for one hundred deliveries. The School-in-a-Box Kit, which I had seen used under a tree in the child-friendly village outside the Darfur camp, contained exercise books, pencils, erasers, and scissors, a wooden teaching clock, a windup solar radio, and other supplies suitable for a teacher and forty students. Other kits included an HIV exposure kit, a basic first-aid kit, a kit with tests to diagnose common illnesses, a cooking kit, a water kit, a recreation kit, and an arsenic-testing kit.

We ended our tour and met up with guests from the United States whom I had invited, including a senior executive at United Parcel Service. Even he was impressed by the multitude of steps UNICEF had to manage in order to address the needs of the world's children. As our tour guide noted, these steps ranged from determining what products are needed, to selecting which of the many types of products are suitable for a particular place or situation, to assessing whether the products available will work in a particular situation (i.e., trying to install water pipes in a war zone), to balancing the cost of products with our ability to afford them, to knowing whom you need to collaborate with in order to get supplies from point A to point B, to finding the financial wherewithal to make it all happen. Other issues existed, too, like keeping items that needed refrigeration cold when children in need lived in extremely hot climates, or their communities lacked the electricity to run a refrigerator, or their homes were so remote that materials had to be carried by hand for long distances. The challenges were endless and required constant innovation. Every link in this chain was vital to the efforts of saving, protecting, and ensuring children's development.

The logistics were fascinating, but the press corps was congregating outside the building, and feeling curious, I went outside to watch them set up. I saw television news trucks and cameramen from European and international organizations jockeying for position with the print and online reporters, each staking out spaces in back of the building, where the royals would exit for a brief press moment. I myself was scheduled to speak with a team from CNN International before proceeding back inside to a specially designated room for a host of print media interviews. Still recovering from jet lag, I brushed my hair, put on fresh lipstick, and mentally prepared myself to step before the cameras.

The interview went well, our conversation covering some basics about the difficult situation in the Horn of Africa and how UNICEF was responding. According to the UN Office for the Coordination of Humanitarian Affairs, this impoverished region was facing the most severe food crisis occurring anywhere in the world. To blame were two consecutive failed rainy seasons, price increases of up to 200 percent for some of the very basic staple foods, and escalating violence in Somalia. Around 3.5 million people in Kenya, 2.85 million in Somalia, and 3.2 million in Ethiopia were in urgent need of humanitarian assistance, in addition to 117,000 people in Djibouti and 600,000 in northern Uganda. These numbers sounded big, but in truth I had trouble conceptualizing them. I tried to think of visual equivalents. How many soccer stadiums full of people did this represent? The soccer stadium in Barcelona, where I had recently attended a game, held around 100,000 people. We now had ninety-six or ninety-seven Barcelona stadiums full of starving people—almost too horrible to contemplate.

As I told CNN, helping these people would be a monumental task, requiring more than just nutrition. Severely malnourished children are nine times more likely to die from infectious diseases such as measles, cholera, and malaria than healthy children. Already, measles cases in the Horn of Africa had increased dramatically that year. UNICEF's response

had to include a variety of supports for children—and thanks
to the supplies we were shipping that day, it would.

We wrapped up, and I went inside for the print interviews. I was still in the room an hour later discussing the
food crisis and how people could help when the whole building fell into a reverential quiet. This could mean only one
thing: the royal couples had arrived. As UNICEF later reported, the royals were issued UNICEF bright blue hardhats
(cyan blue is UNICEF's official color) and were welcomed
by Shanelle Hall, director of UNICEF's supply center. The
duchess and the crown princess were each given flowers by
Amanda Kofoed and Maryam Abdullah, children of UNI-
CEF staff. Both couples received a briefing on the desperate
situation in the region from Peter Hailey, chief of nutrition
for UNICEF in Somalia. He told them that many children
and their parents often have to walk for as many as twenty-
five days to find food. As the visit continued, the royal couples
saw for themselves how the lifesaving aid supplies, including
essential medicines and emergency surgical equipment, were
sourced and packed for shipment to East Africa. The couples
joined UNICEF staff on the packing line and helped to pack
boxes of emergency health kits, each of which would provide lifesaving supplies to over a thousand people. They then
toured the warehouse, seeing the huge variety of supplies
sent to emergencies around the world.

Finishing my press duties, I went to another small room
to meet the royals. My job was to greet them as they came
into the room and then to walk them down the line of guests,
introducing them to the ABC news team, Peter Lamm, and
the private individuals I had invited as a way of thanking
them for making significant donations to UNICEF's food
crisis response. My UK colleague would introduce his guests,

and we would all have a brief chat with the royal couples while enjoying lemonade and cookies.

We made small talk for half an hour. Then the room grew quiet and a young couple walked in, he in a navy velvet blazer, shirt, tie, and slacks, she in a buttoned-down shirt and wool black-and-white-plaid trousers. They weren't the Duke and Duchess of Cambridge. The woman had striking eyes and long dark hair, her partner an easy smile. Who were they? The man caught my eye and said hello, holding out his hand. "Hello," I responded, shaking his hand.

Someone behind me said, "Wow, that's Crown Princess Mary and Crown Prince Frederik of Denmark."

I was so embarrassed! All this preparation as to how to greet a royal, and I had failed to find out what they looked like. I managed to catch myself, and as the prince introduced me to the princess, I smiled and said, "I am so honored to meet you both."

I was walking them down the line of Americans when the room grew very quiet again. The Duke and Duchess of Cambridge had joined us.

Turning the Danish royals over to my UK colleague, I approached the duke and duchess. I couldn't believe how beautiful the duchess was in person. She wore black suede boots and a scarlet dress cinched at the waist with an equally tasteful scarlet belt, the dress and belt matching her husband's tie and the poppy flower pinned to his lapel. I expected our meeting would be a strictly formal affair, so imagine my surprise when Prince William greeted me with a simple and easy "Hi." His smile was absolutely contagious, and he put us all at ease.

We compared notes on Kenya, with Prince William recounting how special the country was to both himself and his wife. I told them about the U.S. Fund's role in the operation, sharing with him how hard the fund had been working to draw attention to the plight of Africa's children. In recent weeks, I had become frustrated that the majority of Americans seemed to be ignoring the huge loss of life. A *New York Times* article in early August had quoted me as saying, "I'm asking myself where is everybody and how loud do I have to yell and from what mountaintop? The overwhelming problem is that the American public is not seeing and feeling the urgency of this crisis." As I explained to the duke and duchess, their participation in the packing of supplies for East Africa's children was important because it drew America's attention, and the world's. I was proud to stand with them.

As we continued to chat, I found myself truly impressed with the duchess. Her grace was matched only by her warmth and beauty. She asked real questions about the food crisis and conveyed her concerns for children. She knew that over 320,000 children were suffering from acute malnutrition, a condition that places the child's life in immediate jeopardy, and that if we didn't raise the money to save these children, they would die. She commented on how shocking these numbers were and asked questions about my experiences visiting other countries to see UNICEF's work. I could tell that her visit today meant something to her—that it wasn't just another charity obligation. She praised UNICEF's work and noted how proud she was to be part of the effort.

Our half hour with the royals seemed to fly by. Soon they were heading out the door to depart for the airport. Even the most cynical among us had been captivated by their presence.

As soon as they left, Peter, the ABC team, and I headed outside, joined by members of my New York team, to find taxis to the airport. Copenhagen was closing down streets to allow the royal motorcade to get through, and we needed to be close behind if we wanted to get there in time to board the plane that would take us (but not the royals) to Nairobi. Unfortunately, our promised taxis were nowhere in sight. I panicked, and my New York team members worked the phones ordering us new ones. It felt like forever, but eventually the cars came and we raced off.

We had been instructed to go to the British Airways ticket counter, where someone would be waiting for us. Because of our delay, this person was no longer there. "Do you have tickets?" the clerk on duty said. When I explained that we didn't, and that we were expecting another staff member to let us through for a UNICEF flight to Nairobi, she said, "Well, I don't know anything at all about that. What's your flight number?"

I glanced at my watch, trying as best I could to contain my anxiety. "We don't have one. This is a special flight. It's not a commercial flight. We need to get through to meet with the duke and duchess. If we don't get through now, we'll miss both them and the flight. It's very important that we're on that plane."

The clerk glared impatiently at me. "That sounds like a likely story. Now I think I've heard it all."

"I'm serious. This is real. Look, check my business card. I'm here with the UNICEF supply mission."

She looked at my card and then at my passport to check that I was the person named on the card. It didn't matter—she just shrugged. "All I can say is you'll have to hold on while I try to confirm this."

We waited for what seemed like forever. I kept glancing at my watch, fearing we'd miss the takeoff.

The woman returned. "I wasn't able to confirm this flight you say you are on."

I was about to explode. "Look, we just came from a special event with the Duke and Duchess of Cambridge. Now we're supposed to help them finish loading the plane. And we're going to Kenya to deliver aid to people in need. Once the royals finish their tour, the plane is going to take off."

She nodded, as if she heard things like this all the time. "Back up and tell me why I don't see this alleged flight on the board. All of our flights go up on that board."

I explained yet again in more detail why we were there and why she could not find the flight on the list of commercial flights scheduled for that afternoon. I also repeatedly tried calling my UK colleague, David, who had accompanied the duke and duchess to the airport, but my calls went straight to voice mail. My patience was wearing thin, and were it not for Peter's reminders to breathe, I don't know what I would have done. We had come all this way to join this flight and deliver the aid in person; I couldn't imagine missing that.

My phone finally rang. It was David. "Where are you? Hurry up! Don't you realize that the royals are finishing up and we're about to take off?"

"We're stuck here. They won't give us tickets to get through security. Can you help us?"

"I'm on the plane. I can't do anything from here. Try to work it out. Look, I've got to go. I'll call you right back."

"But David, the only people who know about this are with you."

He had already hung up, and I was forced to go back to wrangling with the clerk, who by this time had brought two of her colleagues. We learned that nobody had been told about the flight because of security concerns. And I was right: the British Airways executives who had been fully briefed on this mission and who had the gravitas to break through these roadblocks were all on the plane, showing the duke and duchess how and where the supplies were packed.

I'm not sure how, but we finally worked out what it would take to get the ticket counter to issue papers to get us through security, out onto the tarmac, and onto the plane. We had ten minutes left until the official takeoff time air traffic control had given us. We cleared security and ran to catch up with the employees who would take us onto the tarmac. As we neared the plane, David finally called back, letting me know that the royals had already left. This was disappointing, but we were so happy just to be making the flight that we didn't care. Peter, myself, the ABC team, a representative from our supply division, and the airline personnel were soon seated on the mammoth 747, its cargo hold and overhead compartments filled with forty-five metric tons of supplies.

Having spent so many long hours on airplanes, it felt wild to be one of only about a dozen people on board an entire 747. When we reached our cruising altitude, we unstrapped ourselves and behaved like children, running in the aisles and laughing while we plopped into those special business class seats that faced one another. We had dinner together as a group, and as I sat there eating, I could barely believe we had left New York only twenty-four hours before. In one day, we had crossed an ocean, toured our facility, met the Prince and Princess of Denmark, met the Duke and Duchess of Cambridge, raced through the streets of Copenhagen, talked our way through an airport, and were now en route to the Horn of Africa with lifesaving supplies. We were giddy—partially from exhaustion and partially from the knowledge that what we were doing would help children in several countries.

The flight personnel took great care of us, providing us with food, wine, candies, and conversation. We talked about our jobs, our families, what movies we had seen lately. Eventually the conversation turned to Kenya. "Will you be taking all of the supplies with you as soon as you land?" one of the crew asked.

"No," I told her, "The boxes will be held to clear customs first. The Kenyan government needs to check the boxes and ensure we are bringing in what we say we are and that everything is legal. We brought a small amount of nonfood materials with us in our personal luggage and in a few boxes identified as personal possessions—enough for our first delivery. These only need to clear customs with us as we pass through, so they'll be ready for us to deliver quickly and in person. Plus, our UNICEF Kenya colleagues will meet us with nutritional supplements that we will also deliver."

A look of satisfaction and even envy flashed on her face as she thought about what my UNICEF colleagues and I had come to do. It was the first really serious moment since we'd gotten on the plane, and it was obvious she was asking herself a question I posed often to myself: "How is it that I'm so lucky as to be able to play a small role in actually saving children's lives?" The word I use to describe this privilege, corny as it sounds, is "blessed." I feel blessed to have been given the opportunity to fulfill my role at the U.S. Fund for UNICEF, and I think about this blessing almost every day when I come to work.

Until now, the biggest way I contributed was by raising money in the United States to benefit children. On this trip, for the first time, I would enjoy the even greater blessing of being part of the team that physically brought lifesaving tools to people in critical need. I would come away having seen the entire circle, from promoting the cause, to raising the dollars, to acquiring the supplies, to packing them up, to serving as the delivery agent, to finally seeing aid administered. I was elated just thinking about it.

And I was sleepy, too. With just a few hours left of our thirteen-hour flight, the crew gave us blankets and pillows, and before they could finish turning the lights down, we were fast asleep under their watchful eyes. I don't remember exactly what I dreamed, but I do remember feeling very excited, and fulfilled, and happy. It was one of the most memorable and pleasant flights I have ever taken.

We were awakened by the pilot's voice over the loudspeaker telling us it was time to land. He read the usual message about returning our seats to the upright position, putting away carry-on bags, and buckling up in preparation for landing, and then added a special thank-you to UNICEF and to each of us for what we were doing to save children. "We at British Airways are inspired by your example and proud to be associated with this effort. And I'd also like to extend a special thanks to the crew. You have given of yourselves, volunteering to use your vacation time to take part in this mission. I am so proud of your generosity of spirit."

"Is that true?" I asked the flight attendant standing near my seat. "You're all using vacation time?"

She nodded. "The pilot and copilot, too. We're flying there and then turning right around and coming back."

I couldn't believe it. Not only had the crew taken great care of us; they too were part of the mission. I looked up to see tears streaming down their faces, and I was so moved by the pride they were feeling.

The landing was smooth. Although it was 4:00 a.m. local time, we had no sooner come to a halt than our UNICEF Kenya colleagues opened the door and joined us on board. My dear friend Elhadj As Sy, the man leading UNICEF's response for the entire East Africa regional crisis, was first. He stands over six feet tall and carries himself with assurance and grace. He does not speak loudly but with a clarity and conviction that makes you want to listen. He wrapped me in his arms, hugged me tight, and whispered, "Thank you, my sister."

A flurry of activity followed. We pitched in to empty boxes from the overhead bins and pass them up the aisles, one by one, so that they could be handed to other people outside. When this work was finished, Peter and I deplaned, greeting the ground crew and other UNICEF colleagues we'd not yet met. It was still dark outside. The air was misty and warm and heavy with jet fuel, although ours appeared to be the only active plane in the area.

Standing on the tarmac looking up at the 747, I got a sense of just how huge these aircraft are. One of the members of the flight team asked if we wanted to see the plane's storage hull. "Yes, absolutely," I said, without a thought as to how I would get inside it. Peter grabbed my hand, and we jumped onto a forklift, snapping pictures as we rose into the air. I knew my kids would laugh when they saw us on the lift!

The plane seemed even bigger standing inside its belly. I had always imagined the hull of a jet as cramped and low-ceilinged, but it was neither; we were able to stand upright with several feet remaining above our heads. The space was well lit, and several people were moving in and out of it at once. I couldn't believe the amount of aid we had brought—boxes upon boxes, some marked with a list of their contents, others only numbered, but all bearing the UNICEF name on their side.

The unloading seemed to go on forever. As the crews worked, the ABC news team captured it all on tape, while others of us snapped personal photos on our cell phones. The news team asked questions and conducted interviews on the tarmac, all the while taking care not to interfere with the work at hand. Each box was handled as if it were the only box, so precious were the lifesaving supplies contained within. It took us until dawn to unload the cargo that would need to clear customs and also carry away the boxes we planned to hand-deliver.

Without taking time to rest, Peter, the news team, myself, and reps from the UNICEF Kenya team boarded a small propeller plane that would fly us up to the Turkana region in the northwestern part of Kenya, where we would deliver the items we had personally brought, as well as the supplies from our Kenya office. Most of Turkana's 800,000 residents live on less than $1 a day. Few have access to clean water. Medical care is minimal—a doctor for every 50,000 people (as compared with a doctor for every 270 people in the United States). The poverty in Turkana is long-standing, but recent political unrest in Somalia has only made it worse, especially for children. We might have wanted to deliver aid in person to impoverished areas of Kenya along the Somali border, but it was too unsafe to go there, much less to enter Somalia itself. In Turkana, the needs were great and the travel far safer.

Terrified of small planes, I kept telling myself to breathe as we taxied down the runway and took off. One of the people from the news team nudged me with her elbow. "Are you scared too?"

"Totally. You?"

She forced a laugh. "Absolutely."

"Here," I said, grabbing her hand. "Stay with me. How weird that two people like us fly all the time, and we feel this way!"

Peter laughed at my white knuckles, while I held hands across the aisle, each of us doing our best to calm the other down.

It got easier after we reached cruising altitude. We received a briefing from our UNICEF colleagues, a welcome if difficult distraction. Hearing more data about the sheer quantity of people starving, and again feeling overwhelmed and even a bit numbed by the abstract numbers, I found myself thinking of one person, a Somali woman who I'll call Ayan whom my colleague Lisa Szarkowski had told me about. Ayan, who lived in southern Somalia's Gedo region, was pregnant, abandoned by her husband, and lacking any means of earning a living. She decided to leave Somalia, setting out on foot to Kenya with six other families. The group walked for twenty-eight days, covering 420 kilometers, before finally reaching Dadaab, home to the world's largest refugee settlement.

Ayan's journey had been almost unimaginably arduous. Lisa described heavy winds ripping through open fields and covering people with dust, making it hard to breathe. I had shuddered as she mentioned dead animal carcasses littering the land between dried-out and dead bushes. I could almost feel the blistering heat and understand why it was so difficult for anything to survive there. Fortunately, Ayan's story had a happy ending. She had gone into labor, screaming and moaning while lying on the hot sand, when she was found by a UNICEF-trained worker. The worker grabbed a birthing kit from her jeep and helped Ayan deliver a little boy, whom she named Ibrahim.

Flipping through my briefing materials, I came across a similar story, this one originating in Turkana. A woman named Akal Longor had brought her one-year-old son Ekalale to Turkana's Kakwanyang Dispensary and health outreach center. Their entire extended family had traditionally been nomadic pastoralists, moving their herd of goats from place to place in search of land to graze. Over the past few months, the drought had been so severe that the family, along with the other members of their tribe, had become stalled in the desert, losing most of their livestock and lacking money to buy food. As their few remaining goats ceased to produce milk, Ekalale grew weak and became dehydrated. In August, Akal brought him to the outreach center. The team there checked his weight-to-height ratio and measured his mid-upper-arm circumference. As they suspected, little Ekalale was severely malnourished, weighing only five kilograms.

The team placed him in the center's two-room outpatient therapeutic-feeding program, giving him Plumpy'Nut. With malnutrition among the children of the Turkana region running at over 37 percent in some areas, the program and the center itself are godsends. They provide health services that would otherwise require a family to walk four hours to the nearest hospital for care. Ekalale's family got the treatment he needed, returning home between weekly visits. Ekalale had responded well, smiling and even trying to take a few steps when his mother placed him on the ground. His weight had increased to around six kilograms. His acute crisis over, he was slated to receive Unimix, a corn-soya blend, from a UNICEF-supported supplemental feeding program.

Looking out the plane window, I saw a barren desert landscape, not a hint of greenery, only an occasional tree; I couldn't imagine the rocky, hilly land below me filled with grasses for the herds. I leaned over to Peter. "I just read the story of Ekalale. You should read it." I had names to associate with a success story in the region—Ayan and Ekalale—and it helped me gain a perspective on what we had come to do. Still, I pictured the faces of the children who had not been so fortunate, the ones who had perished before the aid reached them, and the ones who would soon perish if we were unable to amass enough resources in time. As I reviewed the many UNICEF reports, I saw one that mentioned six children who had died just the week before because they hadn't made it to the therapeutic feeding center. It was great to read of the successes, but the failures were difficult to digest.

Hearing me discussing Ekalale, one of my UNICEF colleagues commented, "Be careful not to see too much in that success. We need to be cautious; the long-term prospects for children like Ekalale and their families remain uncertain. The droughts come and go, food prices continue to rise, and, as you will see, there is conflict over livestock, water, and other scarce resources in the Turkana region. For children like Ekalale, their timeless way of life is completely uncertain. Many changes are needed."

This led to quite a discussion. For the people of Turkana, the herds of animals that had traditionally accompanied them on their nomadic travels had been more than a source of food; they had formed the center of their social structure and even their complete source of self-identity. These communities

knew no other options. The drought had rendered the pas-
toralist life impossible, but Turkana peoples couldn't simply
embrace modern agricultural or urban existence. Most could
neither read nor write, and they had little exposure to or
understanding of modern practices and technologies. If they
were to move in a different direction, they would require
education. For this reason, UNICEF had placed teachers in
nomadic communities even before the drought had stalled
them. Now, these teachers were setting up semipermanent
schools in locations where the people had set up camp.

As our captain came over the loudspeaker, another UNI-
CEF colleague summarized the situation as follows: "We
have to build on the successes we are having, but ultimately
we must find and create more sustainable solutions." I found
myself whispering "Amen" as we put away our briefing materials, fastened our seat belts, and prepared for our landing
in Turkana.

The drive from the airport was long; the road was filled with
huge potholes that left us bouncing from side to side. Despite
air-conditioning, our jeep was uncomfortably warm because
of the merciless sun bearing down. Looking out the windows, we saw camels wandering the desert and a few small
villages of mud huts with straw roofs. The people were dressed
traditionally, the men and women wearing wraps made of
rectangular woven materials and occasionally an animal skin.
The men's wraps looked more like tunics, one end tied to
the other over their right shoulders. The men wore what
looked like big flat bracelets on one arm; I later learned these
were wrist knives made of steel used to cut hides and other
items. The women wore two wraps, one around their waist,

the other covering their top. The colors were bright, but clearly the clothing was old and worn. Both the men and women had shaved heads; the women often tied beads to the remaining short strands of hair, the men wearing decorative headpieces.

I noticed the men carrying what looked like sturdy polished sticks, with a flat but curved piece running perpendicular at one end. "What are those?" I asked our driver.

He smiled back through the rear-view mirror. "Stools, known as *ekicholong.* The men use them as simple chairs rather than sitting on the hot midday sand. They also double as headrests. When a man wishes to lie down, he uses the *ekicholong* to keep his head off the sand, protecting his ceremonial head decorations from being damaged."

Wow, what a great idea, I thought. The women also wore rows and rows of beads around their necks, layered from chin to chest. These brightly colored beads, juxtaposed against their shaven heads, made their necks appear to be longer than usual, giving them a gazelle-like majesty.

Although I was still very anxious to reach our destination and deliver supplies, I was beginning to feel the lack of sleep and the impact of all-night travel. I tried to keep focused on what we would soon be doing and allow my sheer enthusiasm to keep me awake. Still, I occasionally closed my eyes, only to be awakened by the bumpiness of the road as pavement gave way to dirt, and dirt to sand.

The landscape shifted as we drove, becoming hilly desert. For over an hour, we continued on the road without seeing a single person. Then we mounted a hill and came across a beautiful scene—rays of multicolored light bursting as sun hit the sand, the surrounding hills casting interesting shadows. It took our breath away, a sight so majestic it seemed to have been created just for the purpose of taking unforgettable photographs. The ABC news team asked if we could stop the car so they could capture some footage of the terrain.

We pulled off the road and scrambled out of the cars. The news team busied themselves with the cameras, discussing what they wanted to shoot and from which angle. Peter was talking with our UNICEF friends, and I stood by myself feeling a bit woozy in the heat, my back to a small sandy hill. The air was moving, but the sun was so strong that the breeze provided no relief, and the grains of sand it carried stung my arms and legs. I thought about going back to the jeep, but the motor was off and the air inside even warmer.

I stared at an expanse of empty desert, nothing but rocks and sand, small hills and larger mountains in the distance. There was very little noise, except for the conversations of our group. I am not sure what made me turn around, but as I did, I saw an emaciated woman come over the crest of a hill, holding the hand of a child. Maybe it was a hallucination caused by the heat, but I experienced her appearance in slow motion, at first only seeing her head rising slowly above the sand line, then her body and the child's as she climbed higher and higher. I could not imagine where she had come from, as it had been so long since we'd passed anything that even remotely looked like a habitable place.

I cupped my hand over my forehead to get a better look. I could not decide how old or young the woman was. Her leathery, line-filled skin indicated a lifetime spent under the desert sun. She was very thin; the bones of her arms jutted out from the wrap tied across her top, with the bottom wrap barely able to stay on her thin frame. Her cheeks were gaunt, her eyes almost hollow. The child, whose hand she now held very tightly, seemed equally ageless. Based on her height and size, the child seemed quite young, but when I looked closer, I saw the telltale signs of stunting—a body that just didn't match the maturity of the face.

Who were they? Why were they wandering the desert? Was the woman the mother of this child? The grandmother? Where were they going?

"Hello," I said, fully aware that she likely was not familiar with English. I took a cautious step closer, holding out my hand to her. The woman seemed stunned at my presence. She stepped backward and her eyes narrowed, letting me know that she would defend herself if necessary.

I thought she might turn and run the other way, but she didn't. She seemed to assess me without moving, just staring into my eyes, trying to determine whether it was safe for her to approach. We stood like that for some time, staring deeply at one another, silently testing one another, she on top of the hill, me on the bottom, everyone else so busy they had not even noticed her. The child hid behind the skirt of the woman's wrap, peeking out with half her face.

Somehow the moment passed, and my fears evaporated, as did whatever fierceness I initially perceived in her. We were now connected in some sense—two women who had happened to stumble upon one another. She knew no more about me than I knew about her. Certainly she couldn't have known I was there as part of a relief effort.

Still, her agenda was readily apparent. Still eyeing me, she took her free hand and rubbed her belly. Then she extended her hand to me, like a cup waiting to be filled. She was hungry; she needed help. No matter how frightening my presence may have been, this basic need superseded her fears. The question had been posed: would I help?

During dinner on the plane, I had placed an apple in my

backpack. Now I grabbed it and tossed it to her. She caught it and stared at it in her hand. Her eyes flicked back to meet my gaze. She held that stare for what felt like minutes, although in truth it may have been only seconds. She bowed her head in gratitude, a gesture that left me embarrassed. This piece of fruit that meant so much to her had meant so little to me.

She turned and walked back the other way. I wanted to run after her—to find out more about her, who she was, what had happened to her, where she was going. But just as suddenly as she appeared, she was gone.

We continued on, stopping when we came upon a small community of nomads that had formed into a makeshift village. Aided by a translator, we were able to have the kind of conversations I would have liked to have had with the woman in the desert. Community members described how the initial disruption caused by the drought eventually became devastating as time wore on. Woman after woman told me of days she was forced to choose which of her children would eat and which would not, doing her best to stretch what little sustenance she had. My mind returned to the woman I had just met. Did she have to make similar choices?

We sat in a makeshift classroom that had been set up to help children learn the skills they would need to take on a different way of life. There was one teacher under the thatched roof, held up by three walls made of sticks, open on the fourth side, with more kids surrounding her than I could count, all different ages, all trying to learn to read. We gave out supplies we had brought—pencils, paper, and reading materials—and the children's faces lit up. I smiled as we exited, for the elders—men on one side, women on the other—had placed themselves within earshot. They, too, were trying to learn to read.

Stepping into an open area, we delivered the soccer balls we had tucked into our suitcases. I laughed as I watched Peter teach the game to a group of children who had never seen it played. And then we delivered nutritional supplements to a health clinic where over eighty children were receiving food aid. Seeing those thin children place this much-needed food in their mouths and chew it so intently and happily caused something to shift in me.

I thought back to a dinner I had attended before joining the U.S. Fund. I was breaking bread with the man whose desk I would soon occupy, my predecessor, Chip Lyons, and I asked him why I should want to work for his organization. He responded by listing all of UNICEF's and the U.S. Fund's attributes, describing the challenges as well as the satisfaction I might gain from meeting them. One thing he said stuck with me. "One day you will go to Africa or Asia, or maybe even Latin America, and someone will give you an opportunity to see how what you are doing is actually saving lives. And if you are very lucky, you may someday even get to save a life yourself."

Lo and behold, I had. Chip was right; nothing I would ever do in this job would top this moment. I got to experience the sheer and ultimate joy of seeing a child be given back his life, and of knowing I helped make it possible. But there was something Chip hadn't told me. As wonderful as this moment was, I still had a lingering and discomfiting sense that the satisfaction I felt was somehow hollow. I knew why, too. I couldn't put aside that moment in the desert when I came face-to-face with the starving woman and her child. It was so stark, so simple. That woman needed everything, yet all I had to give her was an apple.

My encounter with this woman had not been planned. It would never be part of a formal report. Perhaps the woman herself would forget it by the next day or would replace it with a memory of some greater effort put forth by someone else. But for me, it was and is everything.

I have thought about that moment many times. I see this woman's face so crisply even as I write these words. The hunger in her eyes, the body so dangerously thin, the hand holding the child so tightly in one hand, the apple in the other. The presence of this woman in my life is why I have written this book. I have also written it because when I go to sleep at night, I see a baby dying in Sierra Leone, groups of children sleeping in the streets, and young girls rushing home to press their shirts under their mattresses. I move about my day knowing that there are thousands of kids like RC who live with HIV/AIDS, and countless others longing to go to school. I see the faces of all the mothers I've met, those whose children UNICEF has helped, and those who could not be reached in time.

I have felt so exuberant seeing Americans come together to support victims of an emergency and experiencing the reward of actually delivering aid. I have also felt thrilled to meet individuals who dedicate their lives every day to helping others, sacrificing their own safety and their time with their families. And I have had the ultimate pleasure of seeing all of this through the eyes of my own children.

Few people get to see what I've seen. My eyes have been opened by the chance I've been given to play a small role in meeting the challenges children confront every day. After six and a half years of bearing witness, I have written this book to fulfill my obligation to the children I've met, ensuring that their stories are told and that they are not forgotten, the meaning of their lives relegated to one of those endless, sad statistics kept about youth.

Mostly, I have written to engage others in the cause. As history has shown, social change requires the involvement of a critical mass of people who see the possibilities and then long for and demand that they be realized. Change requires commitment in our hearts and minds, as well as in our hands and pocketbooks. I hope to someday see everyone in my country on their feet, standing up for the rights of all children, acknowledging what is happening around us and putting an end to anything that denies every child the childhood he or she deserves.

Change will come only if we pursue a multitude of approaches. If you're a writer, write about it. If you're a sculptor, create a sculpture. If you're a parent, teach your children about children's issues. If you have money to donate, donate. Every little bit helps—a mere $1 buys enough good, clean healthy water to sustain a child for forty days. Forty days! Demand that our leaders take positions and allocate resources in a way that puts children first. Use the skills that you have, the voice that you have, the power that you have, on behalf of those who have less.

Read, educate yourself, use technology. Do not wait for someone else to stand up for the children of the world—be that person yourself. Find an image in your own mind that allows you to comprehend just how many children lack what's needed for a healthy, safe childhood. And then, share your awareness with everyone. Let us not stop until we can stand proudly and say that no child is dying from preventable causes; no child has been denied an education; no child has been forced into labor, prostitution, or armed service; and no child has been forgotten by those of us old enough to know better. I believe this is possible. I believe in zero.

NOTES

1. Rosa's Walk

1. A full 69 percent of people in Mozambique lived in poverty in 1992.
2. Project brief, "Example of Strengthening the Service in Health Facilities," UNICEF internal document, 2007.
3. Information in this paragraph taken from internal UNICEF Mozambique document, "Water, Sanitation and Hygiene (WASH) Programme in Urban/Peri-urban Areas."
4. UNICEF Mozambique. "Annual Report 2011 for Mozambique, ESARO."
5. Information taken from project brief, "Chimoio Day Hospital"; "Community-Based Health Activities in Vanduzi, Manica Province."

2. Witnessing Darfur

1. "Internally displaced persons" are people who have been forced from their homes but who remain within their country; "refugees," by contrast, are people who have left their homes and crossed a national border.
2. In October 2012, a mortar shell fell on a regional UNICEF

office, just a few meters away from a room where our staff had taken refuge. Fortunately, the shell did not explode.

3. I Believe in ZERO

1. Tefillin are a set of small black leather boxes tied to the head and arm during prayer, containing scrolls of parchment inscribed with verses from the Torah.
2. In the mother's culture, it is customary to name children on the seventh day after their birth. The mother planned to choose "Fatima" as her baby's name.
3. The majority of mothers and newborns dying of tetanus live in Africa and Southern and East Asia, generally in areas where women are poor and have little access to health care. Data available from 2012 states that 58,000 newborns die each year, that is, one every nine minutes.
4. Although studies showed reductions in infant and under-five mortality, rates were still very high within the region and in comparison with developed countries. Maternal mortality rates were trending downward but still among the highest in the world in 2008.

4. What We Teach Our Children

1. As we did not record RC's speech, I do not have an exact record of what he said. In this chapter, I present my best recollection of what he said and how we responded.
2. These suggestions and examples were taken more or less directly from my previous book, the Anti-Defamation League's *Hate Hurts: How Children Learn and Unlearn Prejudice* (New York: Scholastic, 2000).

6. Respecting Tradition, Bringing Change

1. "Narrowing the Gap to Meet the Goals," UNICEF Report, September 7, 2010.
2. "Despite the global economic crisis, Peru achieved GDP growth

of 7.3% by the end of October 2011, consolidating its status as a middle-income country. Furthermore, the percentage of the population living in poverty continued to decline from 36.2% in 2009 to 31.3% in 2011. Rural poverty declined from 60.3% to 54.2%, continuing the positive trend since 2009." ("Annual Report 2011 for Peru," UNICEF internal report.)

3. *Ibid.*

7. The Bag Makers of Bangladesh

1. "Child Labor in Bangladesh," UNICEF Report, June 2010, http://www.unicef.org/bangladesh/Child_labour.pdf.
2. UNICEF *State of the World's Children Report: Children in an Urban World,* 2012, p. 32.
3. "Progress for Children: A Report Card on Adolescents," UNICEF Report, April 2012, 12–14.
4. *Ibid.,* 8.
5. "Child Recruitment by Armed Forces or Armed Groups," http://www.unicef.org/protection/57929_58007.html (last updated March 22, 2011).
6. "Child Sexual Abuse, Exploitation and Trafficking in Bangladesh," UNICEF Bangladesh Report, 2006, 1–2.

BIBLIOGRAPHY

Published Articles, Reports, Books, and Other Materials

Carter, Rachel Bonham. "Report Finds Nearly Half of All Children in Mozambique Living in Extreme Poverty." UNICEF press release. December 14, 2006.

"Shelling Forces Relocation of UN Staff in Sudanese City of Kadugli." *UN News Centre.* October 9, 2012.

Stern-LaRosa, Caryl, and Ellen Hofheimer Bettmann. *Hate Hurts: How Children Learn and Unlearn Prejudice.* New York: Scholastic, 2000.

"Sudan: Envoy Warns of Ethnic Cleansing as Security Council Calls for Ceasefire." *UN News Centre.* April 2, 2004.

UNICEF. "Narrowing the Gaps to Meet the Goals." September 2010. http://www.unicef.org/publications/files/Narrowing_the_Gaps_to_Meet_the_Goals_090310_2a.pdf.

UNICEF. "Progress for Children: A Report Card on Adolescents." April 2012.

UNICEF. *State of the World's Children Report: Children in an Urban World.* New York: 2012.

United Nations Development Program. "Human Development Report 2009." New York: 2009. http://hdr.undp.org/en/media/HDR_2009_EN_Summary.pdf.

United Nations Security Council. "Report of the Secretary-General on Darfur." S/2006/591, 2006.

Unpublished or Internal Documents

"Bangladesh Field Visit." U.S. Fund for UNICEF. Internal briefing book, February 2011.

"Brazil Field Visit." U.S. Fund for UNICEF. Internal briefing book, August 10–14, 2009.

"Child Labor in Bangladesh." Internal UNICEF report, updated June 2010. http://www.unicef.org/bangladesh/Child_labour.pdf.

"Child Sexual Abuse, Exploitation and Trafficking in Bangladesh." Internal UNICEF report. http://www.unicef.org/bangladesh /Child_Abuse_Exploitation_and_Trafficking.pdf.

"Chimoio Day Hospital." UNICEF project brief. Mozambique, January 2007.

"Community-Based Health Activities in Vanduzi, Manica Province." UNICEF project brief. Mozambique, January 2007.

"Example of Strengthening the Service in Health Facilities." UNICEF project brief. 2007.

"Haiti Field Visit." U.S. Fund for UNICEF. Internal briefing book, October 14–16, 2010.

"Haiti Field Visit." U.S. Fund for UNICEF. Internal briefing book, January 23–26, 2012.

"Mozambique's Invisible Children: Educational Inclusion for Children with Disabilities." Internal UNICEF report, November 2011.

"Peru Field Visit." U.S. Fund for UNICEF. Internal briefing book, August 2010.

"Sierra Leone Field Visit." U.S. Fund for UNICEF. Internal briefing book, September 28–29, 2008.

"UNICEF Annual Report 2011 for Bangladesh." http://www.unicef .org/about/annualreport/files/Bangladesh2010_Final.pdf.

"UNICEF Annual Report 2011 for Mozambique, ESARO." UNICEF.

"UNICEF Annual Report 2011 for Peru, TACRO." UNICEF. http://www.unicef.org/about/annualreport/files/Peru_COAR _2010.pdf.

"UNICEF Annual Report 2011 for Sudan, MENA." UNICEF.

http://www.unicef.org/about/annualreport/files/Sudan_COAR _2010.pdf.

UNICEF Haiti. Consolidated emergency report. March 2012.

UNICEF Mission to Mozambique. Informal presentation. January 2007.

UNICEF Mozambique. Annual Report 2007.

UNICEF Mozambique. "HIV/AIDS & Children Donor Toolkit." 2007.

UNICEF Mozambique. "Thematic HIV/AIDS and Children." March 2012.

UNICEF Sudan. Consolidated Emergency Report 2011. March 2012.

"UNICEF's Work in the Brazilian Amazon." U.S. Fund for UNICEF. PowerPoint presentation. August 2009.

"Water, Sanitation and Hygiene (WASH) Programme in Urban/ Peri-urban Areas." UNICEF internal document.

INDEX